Programming
Made Simple

C Programming
SEXTON
0750632445   1997

C++ Programming
SEXTON
0750632437   1997

Delphi Version 5
MORRIS
0750651881   2000

Delphi
MORRIS
0750632461   1997

HTML 4.0
MCBRIDE
0750641789   1999

Java 2nd Edition NEW!
MCBRIDE, P K
0750653396   2002

Javascript
MCBRIDE, P K
0750637978   1997

Pascal
MCBRIDE, P K
0750632429   1997

Visual Basic Version 6
MORRIS
075065189X   2001

Visual Basic
MORRIS
0750632453   1997

Visual C++
MORRIS
0750635703   1998

ALL YOU NEED TO GET STARTED!

MADE SIMPLE
BOOKS

Basic computer skills

Made Simple

Basic computer skills
Made Simple

Jackie Sherman

MADE SIMPLE
BOOKS

OXFORD · AMSTERDAM · BOSTON · LONDON · NEW YORK · PARIS
SAN DIEGO · SAN FRANCISCO · SINGAPORE · SYDNEY · TOKYO

Made Simple
An imprint of Elsevier Science
Linacre House, Jordan Hill, Oxford OX2 8DP
200 Wheeler Road, Burlington MA 01803

First published 2001
Reprinted 2001, 2002, 2003

TRADEMARKS/REGISTERED TRADEMARKS
Computer hardware and software brand names mentioned in this book are protected
by their respective trademarks and are acknowledged.

British Library Cataloguing in Publication Data
A catalogue record for this book is available from the British Library

Library of Congress Cataloguing in Publication Data
A catalogue record for this book is available from the Library of Congress

ISBN 0 7506 4897 X

For information on all Made Simple publications
visit our website at www.madesimple.com

Typeset by Elle and P.K. McBride, Southampton

Icons designed by Sarah Ward © 1994
Printed and bound in Great Britain

Contents

4 Extra Word features   43

Preface

Although it may seem that everyone else can use a computer and enjoys keeping up with the latest developments, you are certainly not alone if you are new to computers or have some anxiety about information technology.

Sometimes it's the jargon that can put you off, or instructions that are too complicated. Authors of computer manuals may not have actually worked with new computer users and so don't know that it's often the little things that spoil the whole learning experience. This book aims to demystify computers and show you how you can gain the basic skills needed to have confidence and use your computer in exciting and fun ways.

You may have just bought a machine, or need to learn how to use one for work. Perhaps your children are bringing home IT projects and would like your help, or you may want to spend some time e-mailing friends and family abroad or shopping on the Internet for the bargains that are increasingly advertised.

Whatever your motivation, this book will explain what computers are all about and explore the most common applications. With its help, you should be able to produce word-processed documents, prepare illustrated slides to aid your talks or lectures, store and search for information systematically, and handle numbers and charts.

It will also show you ways to access and search for information on the Internet and send and receive e-mails.

Once you have learned the basics, you can turn to other books in the Made Simple series to discover the full power of the applications you have been using.

The examples in this book: they are taken from a computer running Windows 98 and Microsoft Office 2000, as these are now widely in use.

1 Introducing the PC

Hardware

Although this book won't concentrate much on technical aspects, it helps to know a little about your machine so that you can look after it properly and understand terms mentioned later.

The parts of the computer that you can touch and move around are referred to as *hardware*. The components of most importance are shown in the following diagram:

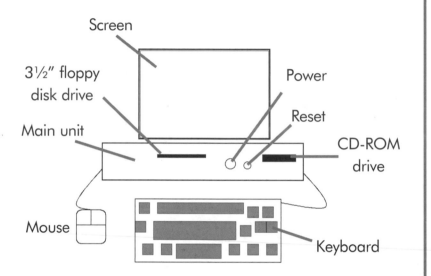

Extra hardware items, *peripherals*, can be added. They include:

Printers – either black and white or colour

Scanners – to allow you to use ready-printed images or written material in your work

Digital cameras – for transferring your own photos into the machine

Other items such as speakers and microphones.

Main components

❑ Screen also known as the monitor or VDU.

❑ Main unit housing processors, memory (RAM) and the hard disk (normally the C: drive). It has a Power On button, and a Reset button for re-starting without turning off the power.

❑ 3 ½" floppy disk drive (normally the A: drive) – the slot for a floppy disk on which you can save your work.

❑ CD-ROM drive (usually the D: drive) – the sliding drawer for a CD- ROM used to play music or games or install new programs.

❑ Mouse – controls a pointer on screen that is used to give instructions to the computer.

❑ Keyboard– for entering text and numbers and an alternative way to give instructions.

Software

The programs that give your computer hardware its instructions and which control everything you see on screen are known collectively as *software*.

Systems software

Starting up when you switch on, checking connections and controlling peripherals such as printers, setting the screen dimensions and colours and allowing you to save or access your work are all activities controlled by systems software. The programs are normally stored on the hard disk inside the main unit.

Applications software

This is software installed on your computer for a particular purpose and is independent of the operating system. Familiar applications include Paint, Word and Internet Explorer.

Applications are commonly installed from a CD-ROM inserted in the D: drive and are then stored on your hard disk. However, the files you create using an application such as Paint or Word can be stored either on the hard disk or on a floppy disk inserted in the A: drive.

Working with software

In Windows, each application is run inside a *window*. You can have several application windows open at the same time and can arrange these in different ways on your screen. To give commands, instead of typing in some obscure programming code, you select from understandable *menus* or pictures of objects – *icons* – found inside the window or on buttons on the *toolbars*.

Take note

Any work you want to keep is saved as a *file*, and some applications have their own names for files e.g. *workbooks* (Excel) or *documents* (Word).

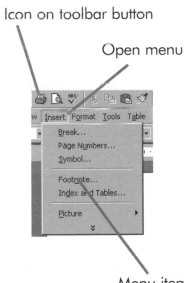

Icon on toolbar button

Open menu

Menu item

Controlling the mouse

For something to happen, you need to give the computer instructions. This can come through pressing keys on the keyboard, e.g. press [Enter] to move the text insertion point down a line or [Delete] to remove an item.

Some of the time you will use the mouse. Roll it gently around on its mat to move a pointer across the screen. When the pointer reaches the target – perhaps a menu option or an open window – you can either press the buttons on the mouse (known as 'clicking') or hold down a mouse button and drag the item to a different position.

The shape of the pointer changes depending on what action it will perform, and you must take care that it is the correct shape before you click or drag. It can be an arrow, hand, cross or vertical beam and the differences will be explained as you go through the book.

Examples of pointer shapes

Browse	? X
Look in: Cursors	

Hand-m	Help_il	Help_rm	Move_l
Hand-r	Help_im	Hourglas	Move_m
Hand-rl	Help_l	Move_1	Move_r
Hand-rm	Help_m	Move_i	Move_rl
Help_1	Help_r	Move_il	Move_rm
Help_i	Help_rl	Move_im	No_1

File name:	Open
Files of type: Cursors (*.ani, *.cur)	Cancel
Preview:	

1 Roll the mouse gently on its mat.

2 Guide the pointer until it rests over the target item on screen.

3 Hold the mouse steady and click the left button once, to select an object or choose an option.

Or

❑ Click the left button twice very fast to double-click and open a window, file or folder

❑ Click the *right* mouse button to open a short menu of options

❑ Hold down the left button as you drag the pointer to move items across the screen

Tip

Double-clicking takes practice. You can often avoid it by selecting an item with a single click, then pressing [Enter].

Basic steps

❏ Shut Down

1 Click the Start button ![Start] in the bottom left-hand corner of your screen and select Shut Down.

2 When you see the Shut Down Windows dialog box, select Shut down.

3 Wait until you see a message that says it is safe to turn off the computer before switching off the power.

4 Click OK.

Like any piece of equipment, a computer needs to be treated properly to offer the best service. That means that certain basic rules need to be followed.

Starting

If the computer is turned off, press the Power On switch. You will need to wait for the system to complete its startup routine.

Away from home, if the computer is shared with others, you may be asked to log in by entering a username and password before you can start work.

A computer that is turned on may show nothing on screen when in power-saving mode, or moving images rather than the normal desktop – the screen saver. To get back to the opening screen, press any key.

Shutting down

Never switch off the power in the middle of your computer session as you can leave the files in a mess and you'll have to wait next time you start while the computer tidies them up for you. Instead, follow the proper shutdown procedure.

Take note

A window that offers choices for you to select or type in, is known as a *dialog box*.

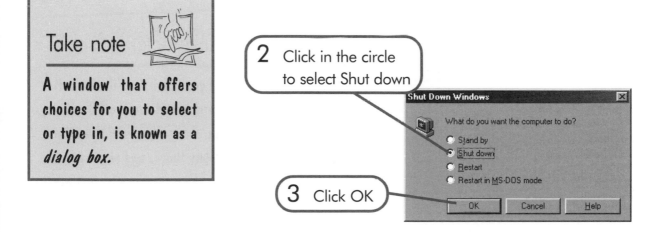

2 Click in the circle to select Shut down

3 Click OK

Restarting

Unfortunately, the computer can sometimes behave badly. It may 'freeze' so that nothing happens when you try to click the mouse or use the keyboard, or the picture may blur or strange windows may open when you haven't done anything.

In these circumstances, it is often best to start again. Without turning off the power completely, you can restart, or 'reboot', the machine and re-open Windows, or just close the particular application you have been using.

You may also occasionally see a nasty notice telling you that you have performed an illegal operation. Don't worry – it usually means you have been trying to do too many things at once. Just click the Close button and re-open your application.

Waitrose

This program has performed an illegal operation and will be shut down.

If the problem persists, contact the program vendor.

Close

Details>>

Close Program

My Documents
Explorer
Microsoft Office Shortcut Bar
Atitask
Directcd
Irxfer
Irmon
Systray
Aticwd32
Apwheel
Apoint

WARNING: Pressing CTRL+ALT+DEL again will restart your computer. You will lose unsaved information in all programs that are running.

End Task   Shut Down   Cancel

(2 Click End Task)

Tip

For details of the keyboard see page 25

1 If the computer is not responding, hold down the [Control] and [Alt] keys with one hand and press [Delete].

2 Click on the End Task option in the Close Down dialog box and you will return to the opening screen.

3 Re-open the application – you may recover your latest piece of work.

4 If something goes wrong but you can use the mouse, go to Start – Shut Down and select Restart from the Shut Down Windows dialog box.

Take note

If you start the PC with a disk in the A: drive the PC will try to find its startup instructions there, and won't be able to. Remove the disk and press any key to start up again.

The Desktop

1   To select an icon, click the left mouse button once when the arrow is directly over it.

2   To open into a window, either double-click the icon or select it and press [Enter].

3   To move an icon on the screen, select it, then hold down the left button with the pointer over the icon, and drag it to a new position.

The opening screen is referred to as the desktop, as visible icons include common office items such as a wastepaper basket (the Recycle Bin) your computer itself (My Computer) and a document folder (My Documents).

Desktop icons represent some of the applications, files and folders within the computer. You can even create your own icons as shortcuts to applications or files you commonly use.

Programs, folders and files all open out as windows that allow you to view their contents and can be moved or resized.

Along the bottom of the screen at all times is the Taskbar. This shows the Start button, needed to launch many of your applications; information such as the time and date; certain shortcuts and any open programs or files in the form of named buttons.

Working with windows

To work with a window you need to recognize the basic parts:

Title Bar: this shows the title of the open file, folder or program

Menu Bar: this is where you'll find menus you can open by clicking the menu name

Toolbar: click the buttons for common actions

Status Bar: this may show certain details, e.g. about the contents of the window.

Scroll Bars: drag the grey box or click the arrows to move the window contents horizontally or vertically.

Control buttons: use them to close or resize the window

To close a window, click ☒ **Close**.

To resize the window, switch between the two interchanging buttons next to the **Close** button: 🗗 **Restore** reduces the size so the Desktop is visible; and 🗖 **Maximize** fills the screen completely.

To reduce the window to a button on the Taskbar, out of the way but easily re-opened with one click; click ▬ **Minimize**.

❑ To change a window manually

1 Click the Restore button.

2 To resize, click and drag any edge or corner in or out when the mouse pointer moved gently over it changes to a 2-way arrow.

3 To move a window, click in the title bar when the pointer shows a white arrow, hold down the mouse button and drag to a new position.

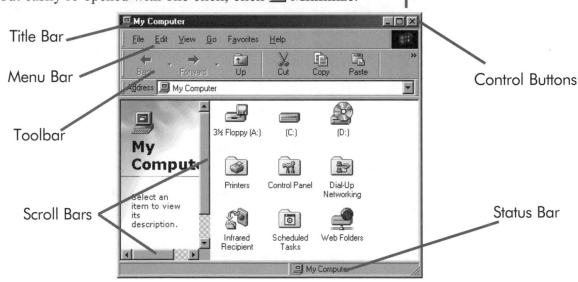

Title Bar

Menu Bar

Toolbar

Scroll Bars

Control Buttons

Status Bar

Customising the Desktop

1 Select Start – Settings – Control Panel - Display and click the Background tab to change the background colour or patterns.

2 To change the screen saver, click the Screen Saver tab and then click the arrow by the Screen Saver box to drop down a list of possible choices.

3 Select a title to see a sample, and click Preview to run it for a short time on screen.

4 Exit the screen saver by moving the mouse or pressing a key, then set the Wait time to elapse before the screen saver comes on, or set other options such as text or colours by clicking the Settings button.

5 Click Apply then OK to save your settings and close the Properties dialog box.

The Task Bar displaying the **Start** button is always visible as it is so important when working with the computer. Clicking the **Start** button offers various choices – to create a new Office file, to launch an application, to find a file or open one you have worked on recently, to get help on Windows, to run a program e.g. from a CD-ROM, or to change basic settings.

When you select **Settings** from the **Start** menu, one option is to customize the look of your Desktop. Click on **Control Panel** and you will see labels for various items such as Date/Time, Keyboard, Mouse, Regional Settings and Sounds. Double click or select and press [Enter] to open any item. A Properties dialog box will appear where you can alter the settings.

Display allows you to change colours or show patterns or pictures as the *wallpaper* that forms the background to your Desktop, or choose from a range of moving images, *screen savers*, which run when you temporarily stop working.

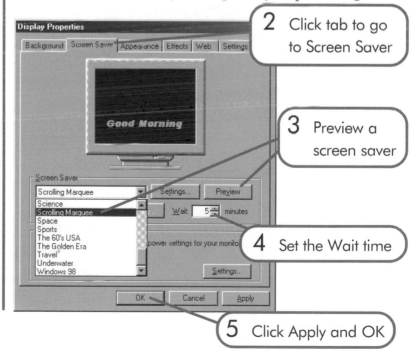

2 Click tab to go to Screen Saver

3 Preview a screen saver

4 Set the Wait time

5 Click Apply and OK

Opening an application

If you have the appropriate icon on the Desktop, double click to open the application. Otherwise, find it listed amongst the programs on your computer. Open each menu in turn and work through the lists until you reach your chosen application. A final click will launch the program.

3 Slide over to the next menu

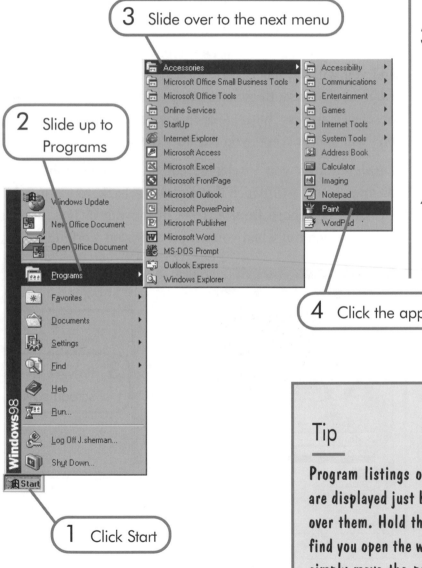

2 Slide up to Programs

4 Click the application

1 Click Start

Basic steps

1 Click the Start button at the bottom, left of your screen.

2 Slide the mouse pointer up the list that appears and rest on *Programs.*

3 Slide across to the next menu and select an application e.g. Microsoft Word, or an option e.g. *Accessories* to open a further menu.

4 Click an application and it will launch to display its opening screen

Tip

Program listings opened via the Start button are displayed just by resting the mouse pointer over them. Hold the pointer steady or you may find you open the wrong menu. If this happens, simply move the pointer and try again.

Looking after yourself

1 Avoid eating and
drinking near the
keyboard, as liquids
and sticky crumbs will
ruin its efficiency.

2 Keep any cables or
bags well out of the
way, so there is no
tripping up as you rush
to the printer or to
answer the telephone.

3 Shut down the machine
correctly, rather than
turning it on or off like
a light switch.

When working with computers, there are simple rules to follow
that will minimise any risk to your health.

Get comfortable

Make sure your chair is at a comfortable height and supporting
your back, and adjust the monitor so that your eyes are broadly
level with the top of the screen. If you can, make use of
document holders, footstools or wrist supports to aid your
comfort. You may also want to ensure you have plenty of room
to move your legs freely.

Take breaks

Take frequent, short breaks to stop yourself sitting too long in
one position.

Watch your eyes

Adjust the screen or window blinds to reduce glare, and stop
working if you get a headache or fuzzy vision.

Adjust equipment

Try to keep a light touch on the mouse, position the keyboard
so that it is comfortable to use and keep a good working space
round you. Adjust screen settings using buttons on the monitor
for maximum clarity and restful colour contrast.

Tip

**If you still have trouble
after taking sensible precautions, do see your
doctor or optician.**

Summary

❑ Any parts you can see and touch are computer hardware whereas sets of instructions written as programs and stored on disks are called software.

❑ The opening screen is called the desktop and it displays small icons representing the programs and files in the computer. Each program runs in a window that can be re-sized and moved using buttons or the mouse pointer.

❑ You can customize your Desktop via the Control Panel, and find programs from the Start menu, opened by clicking the button at the bottom of your screen.

❑ You should always shut down the computer properly, rather than simply turning off the power.

❑ It is important to take sensible precautions when working at the computer, to maintain your health and safety.

2 Getting organized

Where's that file?

After working on a computer for even a short time, you could well have saved a number of pieces of work, known as *files*, on disk. Each time you want to find a particular file, you'll have to scroll through a growing list of names – a time-consuming and inefficient system.

Instead, you can group your files into labelled folders, rather like drop files in a filing cabinet, so that all you need do is open the relevant folder and search through a limited number of files to find the one you want.

You can either manage your files from the desktop, or use the file management program – *Windows Explorer*. Whichever system you use, you can create as many folders as you need and then move or copy files between them.

The folders structure

A disk is known as the root directory or folder and is represented by the disk drive letter. (C:) represents your hard disk and 3½" floppy (A:) represents a floppy disk in drive A.

Folders and subfolders form a hierarchy, or the branches of your directory/folder 'tree', so that a folders structure can look something like this:

Take note

You need to be able to tell the difference between icons for folders and files

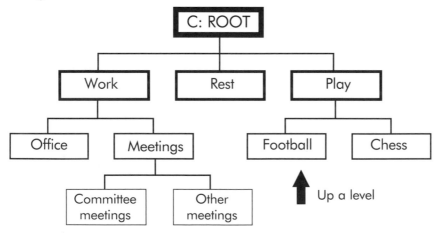

Basic steps

1 Choose Windows Explorer from the Start – Programs menu.

2 Select the disk or folder in the left pane in which to create the folder.

3 Go to File – New, click Folder and wait a few seconds.

4 When a new folder appears in the right pane, type a name into the box over the high-lighted words *New Folder*, and press [Enter].

❏ Made a mistake? Select the new folder and then *right*-click to produce a short menu. Select Rename and edit or retype the name.

Take note

In Windows Me, see the Explorer panes by click-ing the Folders button in My Computer.

Exploring folders

When you open Explorer, you'll see a window with two panes – in the left the folders structure of your computer, and in the right the first level of contents of any selected folder. The address box shows which folder is open at any time and you can click the name of a folder in either pane to view its contents.

If items have + next to their name in the left pane, it means they contain folders. Click the + to expand the structure. Click the symbol again (now -) to return to the root folder.

Creating a folder

Select the location in the left pane (you may need to click + to reveal a particular folder) and then use the **File** menu options to create your folder.

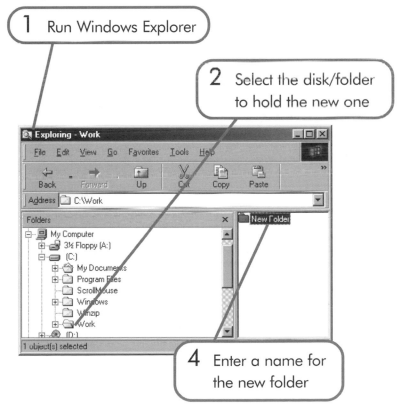

1 Run Windows Explorer

2 Select the disk/folder to hold the new one

4 Enter a name for the new folder

Filing

Once you have created one or more folders, you can reorganize your files *as long as they are closed*. If you see a message saying a file can't be moved, return to the application and close the file before continuing.

Files are moved by dragging them from their original position to the new destination. You can also create a copy of a file in a different folder using this method.

1 Make sure that both the file and the destination folder are visible.

2 Select the file.

3 Right-click on the file and drag it to the destination folder.

4 When the destination folder becomes highlighted, let go the mouse button.

5 Select Move Here to move the original file or Copy Here to place a copy in its new folder.

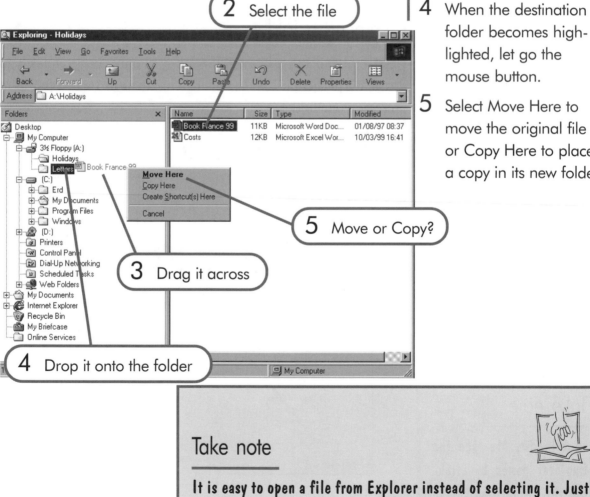

2 Select the file

3 Drag it across

5 Move or Copy?

4 Drop it onto the folder

Take note

It is easy to open a file from Explorer instead of selecting it. Just close the file and return to Explorer by clicking its Taskbar button.

Basic steps

Selecting several files at once

☐ Selecting a range of files

1 Make sure your files are displayed as a list. You can do this by selecting View – List.

2 Click the first file.

3 Hold down [Shift]and click the last file in the range.

All files will now be highlighted.

☐ Selecting non-adjacent files

4 Click the first file.

5 Hold down [Control] and click the other files individually.

6 Drag any file across to the left pane and they will all move together.

To move several files at the same time, you need to use a method that allows you to highlight more than one at a time.

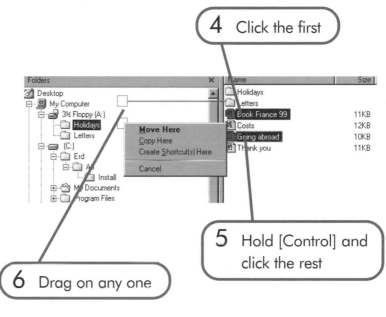

4 Click the first

5 Hold [Control] and click the rest

6 Drag on any one

Take note

If you drag with the left button down, there is no menu when you drop the file. You will always move files within the same drive and copy files between different drives. If you aren't careful, the file can disappear into the wrong folder and you'll need to find it and move it out again.

Folders on the Desktop

It is sometimes simpler to organize folders and files on the desktop rather than opening Windows Explorer. Many of the actions are just the same, but you work with icons or open windows rather than across the right and left panes of the Explorer window.

❏ To create a folder

1 Double-click My Computer to start it up.

2 Open the hard disk (C:) or 3½" Floppy disk (A:) to display the contents.

3 Select File – New – Folder and name the new folder.

❏ To move or copy files

4 Make sure the destination folder is at least partially visible.

5 Select the file(s).

6 Right-click and drag it onto the destination window or until the folder is highlighted.

7 Let go the mouse and select Move Here or Copy Here.

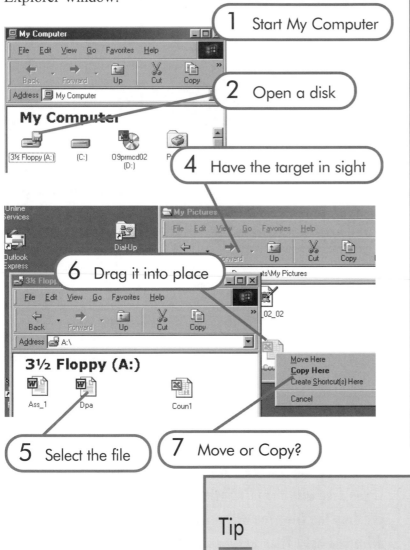

1 Start My Computer

2 Open a disk

4 Have the target in sight

6 Drag it into place

5 Select the file

7 Move or Copy?

Tip

If dragging with the left button, hold [Control] to *copy* files within the *same* drive, or [Shift] to *move* files *between* drives.

Deleting files

1 Select the file and press [Delete].

Or

2 Select the file in the right pane and drag it across to the Recycle Bin folder.

Or

3 Right-click the file and select Delete from the menu of options.

Files that are no longer needed should be deleted to keep your disks tidy. Deleting is quick and easy, and if a file is deleted by mistake, it can be restored to its original location by opening the Recycle Bin, selecting the file and clicking Restore.

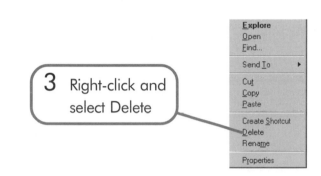

3 Right-click and select Delete

Tip

To delete a folder, first check that it doesn't contain any files or subfolders you wish to retain. If it does, move these out first and then press Delete.

Backing up work

You only have to lose work once to know that it's a good idea to keep a copy somewhere else. Then, if your disk becomes corrupted, you still have a copy of your work available.

Normally, if you save files onto your hard disk, you could keep backup copies on floppies. For a few files, the simplest option is to use Windows Explorer to make copies of your work on a floppy disk in drive (A:) as described on page 16.

To make backups on the hard disk, in case a file becomes unreadable, you could save a second copy, perhaps in a different folder, or there may be an *Always Create Backup Copy* option within the application you are using (one of the **Save** options usually reached via the **Tools** menu). Windows 95/98 users also have a special backup program – *Microsoft Backup* – in the **System Tools** menu.

Cut, copy and paste

When moving or copying files on the Desktop, you may prefer to use the cut/copy and paste method rather than dragging.

Cut places the file in a temporary part of the computer's memory known as the Clipboard, and *Copy* places a copy of the file here, leaving the original in place.

To move the files out of the Clipboard, you have to click *Paste*.

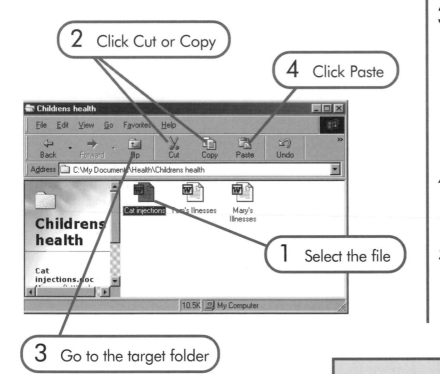

Basic steps

1 Select the file or folder you wish to move or copy.

2 Click the Cut or Copy toolbar button or select these options from the Edit menu.

3 Open the destination window – you may need to go up a level within the present window to move back through the folder's pathway.

4 Click the Paste toolbar button or select Edit – Paste.

5 The original, or a copy of the file will now appear in the selected folder.

Take note

Windows Me has Copy To Folder and Move To Folder commands on the Edit menu and toolbar, which are simpler alternatives to Cut or Copy when working with files.

Formatting a disk

1 Push the disk into the A: drive until you hear a click. The release button will pop out.

2 Open My Computer and select the 3 ½ Floppy (A:) icon then go to the File menu and select Format, or right-click on it and select Format.

3 At the Format dialog box, for the Capacity, accept *1.44Mb* for high-density disks, but select *720Kb* for older double-density disks.

4 Use the Quick option to remove files from an old disk, but Full for an unformatted disk.

5 Click Start and wait for the confirmation that formatting is complete.

6 Close the dialog box or repeat with a new disk.

Before you can save your work onto a floppy disk, it has to be formatted. This lays down the tracks and sectors for storing information correctly. Although you can buy floppy disks ready formatted, sometimes you may need to use an unformatted disk. You may also want to reformat a disk as a quick way to erase unwanted files. As formatting destroys any information previously stored, you NEVER format a hard disk.

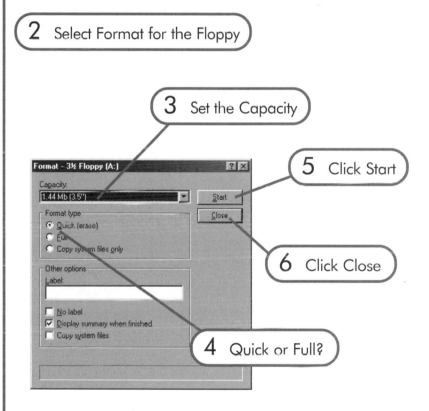

2 Select Format for the Floppy

3 Set the Capacity

5 Click Start

6 Click Close

4 Quick or Full?

Summary

❑ Unless you organize your files when working on the computer, you will find it very hard to keep track of everything you produce.

❑ You can create folders on the desktop or within Windows Explorer that can be used to group similar files together so they can be easily located.

❑ Files can be dragged into folders or placed there using the cut/copy & paste technique, and you can select groups of files to move at the same time.

❑ Take care when deleting folders as they may contain files you want to keep.

❑ It's a good idea to make a backup copy of your work so that losing the original won't be a disaster.

❑ Before you can use a floppy disk, it must be formatted.

3 Simple documents

Opening Word

When you launch Word, the first *document* (the name given to any file produced in Word) always opens directly on screen. It has Document 1 as a temporary title until you save and name it with a more memorable name.

To open subsequent documents, click the *New* toolbar button, or go to **File – New – General** (tab), select *Blank Document* and click OK.

You can open new documents one on top of the other. The names of all open documents other than the top one will appear as buttons on the Taskbar and you can click any button to switch to that document. It will then become the active window.

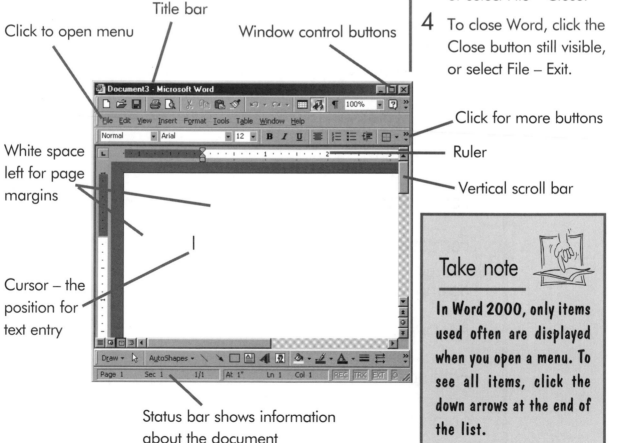

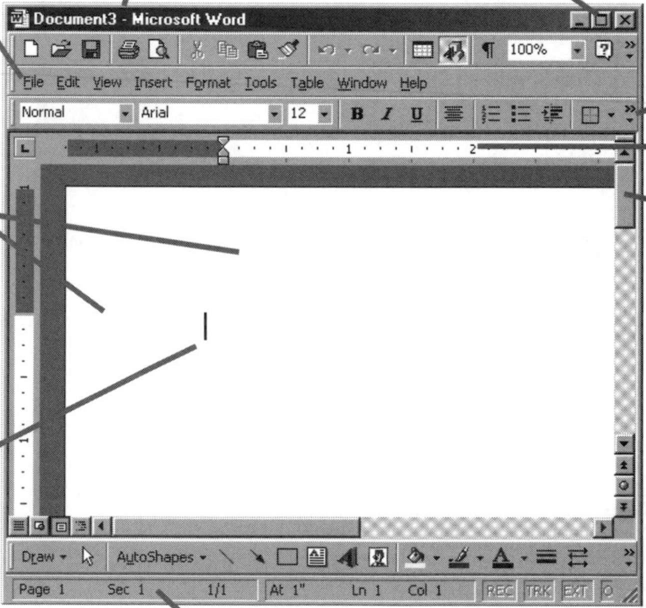
Title bar
Click to open menu
Window control buttons
Click for more buttons
Ruler
Vertical scroll bar
White space left for page margins
Cursor – the position for text entry
Status bar shows information about the document
Document3 - Microsoft Word
File Edit View Insert Format Tools Table Window Help
Normal
Arial
12
100%
Draw
AutoShapes
Page 1 Sec 1 1/1 At 1" Ln 1 Col 1 REC TRK EXT

Basic steps

1 If the Word icon is on your Desktop, double-click it or select it and press [Enter].

Or

2 Click Start, point to Programs and then click Microsoft Word.

3 To close a document, click the Close button or select File – Close.

4 To close Word, click the Close button still visible, or select File – Exit.

Take note

In Word 2000, only items used often are displayed when you open a menu. To see all items, click the down arrows at the end of the list.

Basic steps

1 Press a key to enter a letter, digit or lower symbol, e.g. / or =.

2 Hold down [Shift] to enter capital letters or symbols at the top of the keys, e.g. + or @

3 Press [Caps Lock] to enter a line of text in capitals.

4 Erase text errors to the left of the cursor with [Backspace], and to the right with [Delete].

5 Press [Tab] to move the cursor across the page in jumps of 0.5".

Entering text

When a new Word document opens on screen, you'll see a flashing vertical bar – the cursor – positioned at the top left-hand corner. This is where any characters you type will appear.

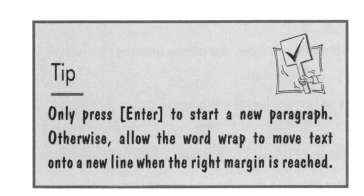

Tip

Only press [Enter] to start a new paragraph. Otherwise, allow the word wrap to move text onto a new line when the right margin is reached.

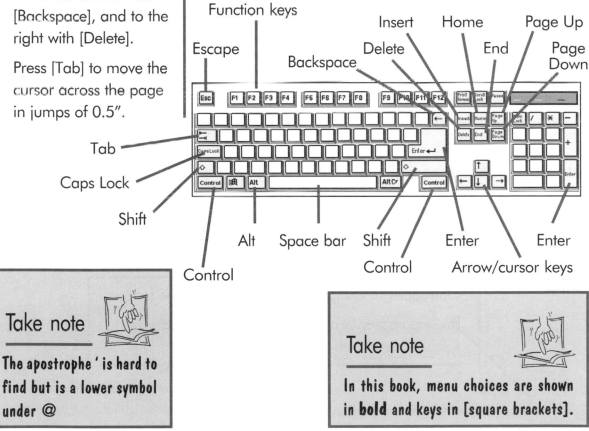

Function keys

Escape

Backspace

Insert

Delete

Home

End

Page Up

Page Down

Tab

Caps Lock

Shift

Control

Alt

Space bar

Shift

Control

Enter

Arrow/cursor keys

Enter

Take note

In this book, menu choices are shown in **bold** and keys in [square brackets].

Moving the cursor

Once you have entered some text, you may need to move to different parts of the document to make changes or add new words.

Using the keyboard

[Enter[will move the cursor onto the line below, creating a new blank line.

The **[arrow keys]** will move it in any direction except below the last line of typing.

[Home] takes it to the start of the line.

[End] takes it to the end of the line.

Hold **[Control]** as you press **[Home]** or **[End]** to go to the start or end of all text that has been typed.

[Page Up] or **[Page Down]** will move through large blocks of text in long documents. You can also click the vertical or horizontal scroll bar arrows in the appropriate direction.

Using the mouse

When the pointer shows a vertical **I**, position and click to place the cursor on the screen. If it is not in exactly the right place, use the arrow keys to move it across one character at a time.

❑ Paragraph changes

1 If the cursor is at the start of a line, pressing [Backspace] will join this sentence up to the line above.

2 If the cursor is at the end of a line, [Delete] will join this sentence to the following line of text.

3 Take care not to split words when you press [Enter] as everything following the cursor will move onto the next line.

Click here to start new paragraph

One sentence is short. **I**Two sentences can be longer.

INew paragraphs are hard to cre**I**ate and easy to split up by mistake.

Click here to split the word

Click here to join sentence to line above

Spelling and Grammar

1 Right-click on the red or green wavy underlined word.

2 To check the whole document, click ✓ to open the Spelling and Grammar dialog box.

3 Select an alternative in the Suggestions pane or edit the mistake.

4 Click Change so that your document will reflect the changes.

5 New words will appear until the checks are complete. Either ignore or alter/replace each one in turn.

6 To leave the checking box at any time, click Cancel.

You may notice that some words you enter become underlined in red or green. Red means Word doesn't have it in its dictionary – often, but not always, because it is misspelt – and green means that it appears to break the conventional rules of grammar.

To check a single word, right-click to drop down a short menu. For selected text or the entire document, click the Spelling and Grammar toolbar button ✓. This will pick up the first underlined word(s) and you can select an alternative, ignore all suggestions or manually alter the words concerned.

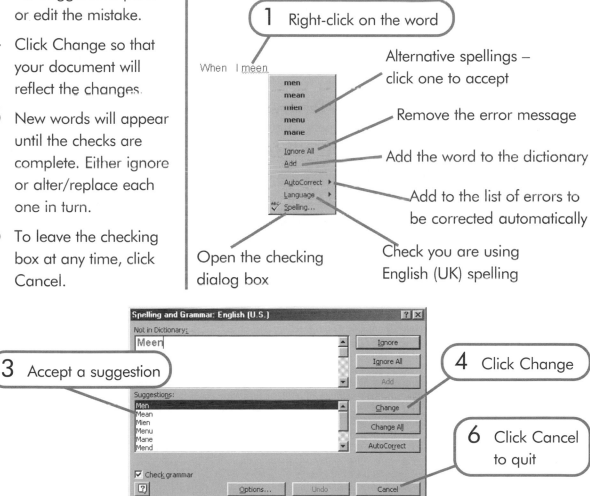

1 Right-click on the word

Alternative spellings – click one to accept

Remove the error message

Add the word to the dictionary

Add to the list of errors to be corrected automatically

Check you are using English (UK) spelling

Open the checking dialog box

3 Accept a suggestion

4 Click Change

6 Click Cancel to quit

Troubleshooting

Everyone presses the wrong key at some time, or makes another mistake that could involve a great deal of re-typing, and so Word gives you useful shortcuts to put things right.

Correcting common mistakes

Undo toolbar button allows you to go back one or more steps and is particularly useful if you delete or move text by mistake.

[Insert] key will return to inserting text between letters if you changed to Overtype mode by accident and find text being replaced.

Close button will return to your work if you opened a new document or dialog box by mistake. This often happens when holding [Control] rather than [Shift] as you type a capital letter (e.g. [Control] + [N] opens a new document, and [Control] +[P] opens the Print dialog box).

View – Toolbars or **Ruler** allows you to locate missing screen items. If a new toolbar appears as a box on screen, click in the blue title bar and drag it up just above the ruler or just below the bottom of your document. When you see it start to lengthen in shape, let go and it will spring into place.

❑   Undo

1   To undo the last action taken, select Edit - Undo or click the Undo toolbar button ⟲ *before* clicking another button or pressing any key.

2   For mistakes made further back, you can step through the changes you made or select past actions from the drop-down list produced by clicking the arrow next to the Undo button.

3   Select Edit – Repeat or the Redo button ⟳ if you go too far.

Basic steps

1 If you select Help –
Microsoft Word Help,
or click the toolbar
button [?], you will
open the main Help
window. You can then
select one of three tabs:
Contents, Answer
Wizard or Index.

2 Select Help – Show
Office Assistant or
press [F1] to get the
'Clippit' helper. You
can type questions or
accept Help on activi-
ties such as writing
letters. The
Office Assistant will
remain available unless
you select Help – Hide
Office Assistant.

If you click the Options
button you can change
the appearance in the
Gallery, adjust some of
its settings or remove
the Assistant altogether.

If you have problems, or want to learn something new, Word
has a range of help functions available on-line. You can view
demonstrations, have your questions answered, display defini-
tions, get step-by-step guidance, trouble-shoot or simply read
about most aspects of the application.

Contents – select topics to display in detail

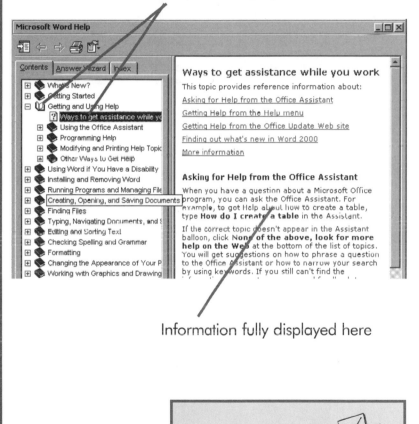

Information fully displayed here

> **Tip**
>
> **If you forget what a toolbar button
> is for, rest the mouse on it and a
> brief definition will appear.**

Answer Wizard – type in questions, click Search and select related topics that you can then display

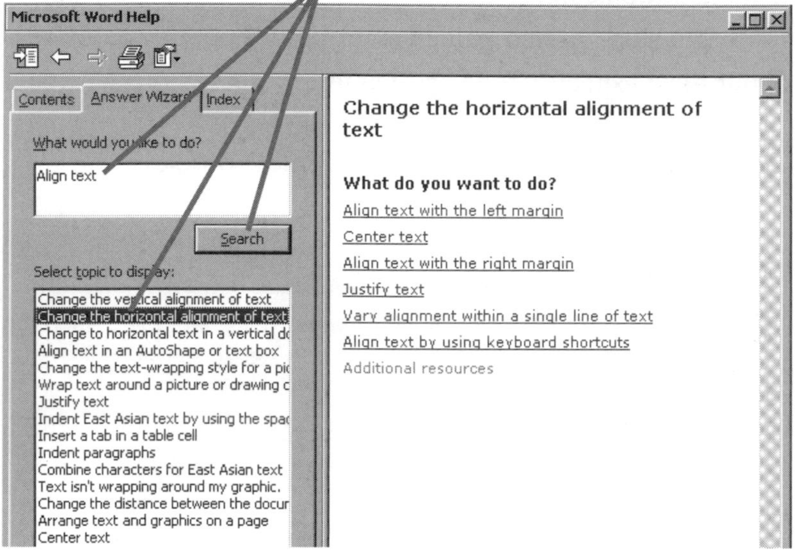

Index – enter key words and click Search or choose from the list to display topics containing those words

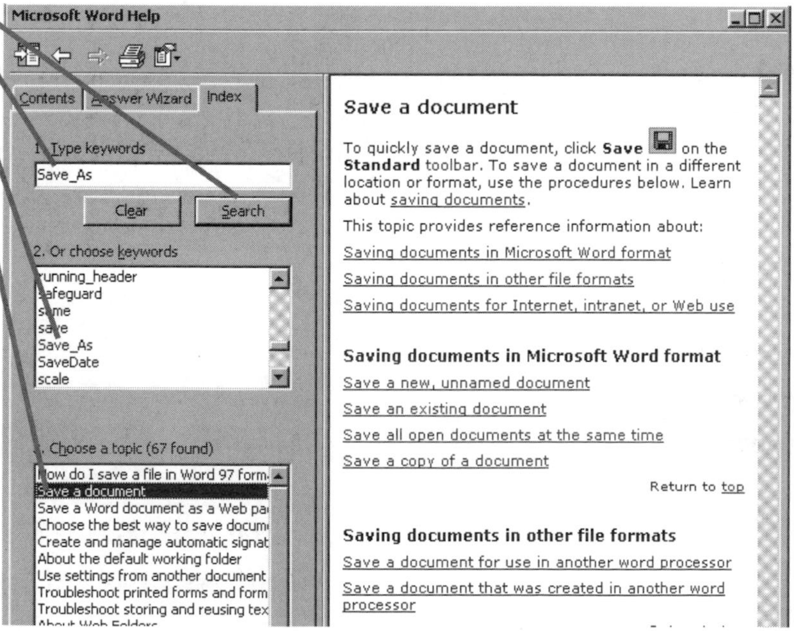

3 Also on the Help menu is *What's This?* Click on this then click a part of the window to reveal a definition.

4 On some dialog boxes there is a question mark next to the Close button that works in the same way as *What's This?*

5 Select Help – Office on the Web when you are connected to the Internet to have access to a vast amount of extra Help and guidance.

Basic steps

Using the mouse

- ❑ Select one word by double-clicking it.

- ❑ Triple-click to select a whole paragraph.

- ❑ To select a block of any size, click at the beginning of text, hold down the button and drag the cursor across to the end.

- ❑ Select a line by moving the mouse pointer in the left margin until it shows a right-facing arrow. Click, or click and drag up or down to select several lines at the same time.

Tip

Select the complete document by pressing [Control] + [A] or go to Edit - Select All.

Each document has pre-determined settings that are known as the *default*, and these include style and size of characters, line spacing, margins and the alignment of entries on the page.

To alter the look of your text, either change these settings before typing, or type the text in the normal way and then go back and make changes to particular sections using the various formatting tools available.

To restrict the changes to certain words or paragraphs, you must select (highlight) them so that the text appears white on a black background. Any new instructions you give the computer concerning changes to characters or paragraphs will now only affect the selected text.

There are many different ways to select entries, using either the mouse or the keyboard.

Click here to select the whole line

Selected text

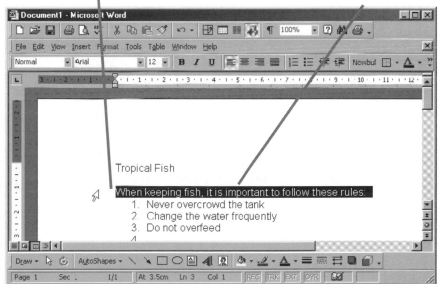

1 Click at the start

2 Scroll down

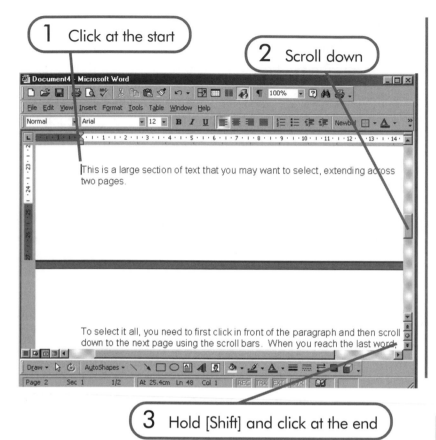

3 Hold [Shift] and click at the end

❑ To select a large block

1 Click at the start of the entry to place the cursor in position.

2 Scroll down to the end of the block.

3 Hold [Shift] and click the button again.

Using the keyboard

4 Move the cursor to the start of text.

5 Hold down [Shift].

6 Press the arrow keys in the desired direction.

Tip

If the black highlight extends too far when selecting text with the mouse, keep the button depressed as you slide the mouse slowly back up the line of text.

Tip

If you press a key when text is selected, it is deleted or replaced with a letter or number. If this happens, click Undo.

To take off the highlight but not delete the entry: click on screen once with the mouse.

Basic steps

- ❑ Click the toolbar buttons to apply bold, italic or underline.

- ❑ To change the font type and size, click the down arrow by the boxes to display a menu from which to choose.

- ❑ Click the arrow next to the Font Colour toolbar button **A** to choose a colour other than black.

- ❑ Styles combine pre-set font and paragraph settings. A range of styles is available from the drop-down list in the Style box.

Formatting means changing the look of your text. There are various toolbar shortcuts for applying different formats to characters. Sometimes they can be clicked on and off (e.g. **Bold** or *Italic*) or one format must replace another e.g. Font (character design) type or size.

Either set the formatting to apply to the text you are about to type, or select existing text and then apply the formatting.

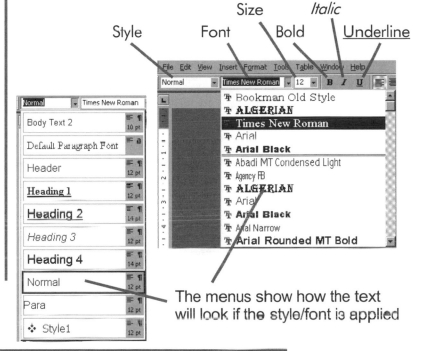

The menus show how the text will look if the style/font is applied

Tip

If you make changes to text once e.g. by applying a style or choosing a new font, save time repeating the formatting elsewhere by 'painting' the changes over text using the Format Painter button. Select an example of the modified text, then click ✎. The pointer will now show a paintbrush. If you drag this across text, the new formatting will be applied automatically.

The Font dialog box

To make detailed changes to the look of your text, you need to go to the **Format – Font** dialog box.

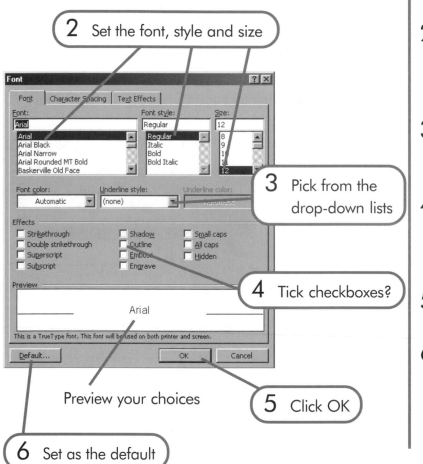

2 Set the font, style and size

3 Pick from the drop-down lists

4 Tick checkboxes?

Preview your choices

5 Click OK

6 Set as the default

1 Select the text then use Format – Font to open the dialog box.

2 Select any font type, style or size and pre-view the effects in the Preview pane.

3 Use drop-down menus to apply special under-lining or text colours.

4 Click in the checkboxes to apply special effects such as shadows or outlines.

5 When you have made your choices, click OK.

6 If you would like all your future documents to have these formats pre-set, click Default… and then click Yes.

Tip

If you type capitals by mistake, select the text and then hold Shift as you press [F3]. You will be offered a repeat of lower case, Sentence Case or UPPER CASE as you press. Other-wise, select the text and then go to **Format – Change Case**.

Formatting paragraphs

❑ Setting alignment

1 Click the appropriate alignment toolbar button.

Or

2 Use the keyboard shortcuts:

[Control] + [L] Left

[Control] + [E] Center

[Control] + [R] Right

[Control] + [J] Justify

In computing, 'paragraph' means any text typed between two [Enter]s on the keyboard. If you want to format a single paragraph, you select it by just clicking somewhere inside. If you want to apply a new format to more than one paragraph, select the relevant block of text with the mouse or keyboard before formatting.

There are toolbar or keyboard shortcuts for changing text alignment, line spacing or indentation, but you can also make these choices via the **Format** menu.

Alignment

One of the most common changes you are likely to make is to the position of text on the page. There are four alignment toolbar buttons:

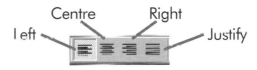

- ● **Left** aligned to line text on the left margin

- ● **Centre** aligned to position text around a central point

- ● **Right** aligned to line text up on the right margin

- ● **Justify** will 'stretch' text across the page and so neaten the right-hand edge. Sometimes too many spaces are inserted, but it can give text a more professional look.

Line spacing

Normally, new lines of text appear one below another with little white space between them. This is *single line* spacing and is the default setting.

If you want more space on your page, you can change to 1.5 or double spacing, or select a specific spacing measurement.

Indenting paragraphs

You may want a paragraph to be set some way in from the left or right margins e.g. so that it stands out or as a way to present quotations in a document.

This paragraph is not indented and so lines up with both the left and right margins in the normal way.

> This paragraph is indented by 0.5" (1.27cms) from the left but not from the right, so that the application of word wrap always leaves a space on the left.

>> This paragraph is indented by 1.18" (3 cm) from both the left and right margins.

❑ Line spacing

1 Hold down [Control] as you press [1] for single, [2] for double or [5] for 1.5 spaced lines.

❑ Indentation

2 To move a paragraph in from the left margin by 0.5", click the Increase Indent toolbar button.

3 Reverse indent by clicking the Reverse Indent button, showing the arrow pointing in the opposite direction.

Basic steps

1 Select Format – Para-graph and click the Indents and spacing tab.

2 To change left or right paragraph indents, select the box and alter the measurement by clicking the up/down arrows or typing in an exact figure.

3 Click the drop-down arrows to see the Line spacing options and select a standard spac-ing or choose Exactly, At Least or Multiple and enter the number in the At: box.

4 Preview the changes you make and then click OK.

The Paragraph dialog box

If you want to set your indents or line spacing more exactly, you can do it from the **Paragraph** dialog box.

1 Go to Paragraph – Indents and Spacing

You can set the alignment here

2 Set the indent amount

3 Set the Line Spacing

Use the Preview as a guide

4 Click OK

Tip

The arrows in measurement boxes move numbers in 10ths, but you must click in the box and alter numbers manually to change measurements by 100ths.

Saving work

After all the hard work of creating a document, you'll want to save it. There are three questions you need to ask:

● Where do you want to save the file? On the hard disk, or perhaps onto a floppy disk you can take with you to work.

● What do you want to call it? When you want your work later – to edit it or print a copy – finding **Technical CV** is going to be far easier than finding **Document 26.**

● Do you want more than one copy? If you need different versions of a CV, for example, you could edit the original and save both **Technical CV** and **Management CV** files.

Basic steps

1 Click the Save button
🖫 or select File – Save
or Save As to open the
Save As dialog box.

2 Select the target folder
from the Save in drop-
down list.

3 Word names files by
entering their first line
of text into the File
Name box. Edit or
replace this name as
appropriate.

4 Click the Save button.

5 To keep your original
unaltered but create a
second copy, use File –
Save As to open the
Save As box and
change the location
and/or rename the file
before clicking Save.

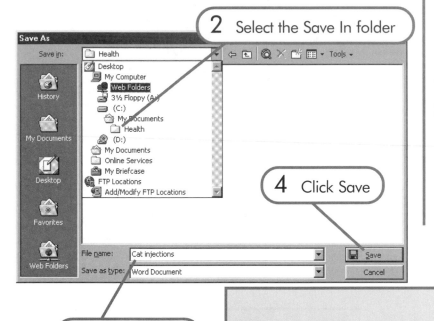

2 Select the Save In folder

4 Click Save

3 Edit or replace the name

Tip

Once you have named a file, update any changes *regularly* by clicking the Save button, so that you do not lose later work if the computer crashes. This will NOT reopen the Save As box, but will resave the file with the same name.

Opening previously saved files

Basic steps

1 Click the Open toolbar button or select File – Open.

2 In the Open dialog box, make sure the correct folder or drive shows in the Look in slot – if necessary, look in different folders by clicking the Up One Level button or opening a folder visible in the main window.

3 Scroll through your files and select the one you want to open.

4 Click the Open button or press [Enter].

The main reason for saving files is so that you can open them again later – perhaps to make changes or to print a copy.

If your work has been saved properly, all you need do is open the *Open* dialog box and scroll through your files until you find the one you are looking for. Select it and click Open and it will appear on screen as the active window.

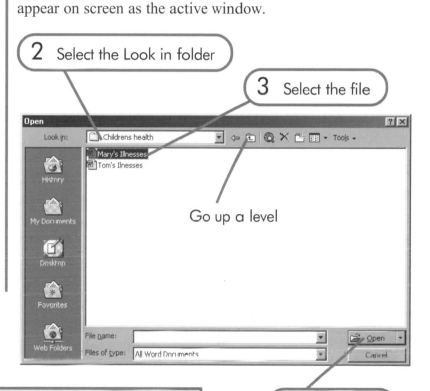

2 Select the Look in folder

3 Select the file

Go up a level

4 Click Open

Tip

When transferring files to a different computer, you may find you cannot open your documents because the machine is running an earlier version of Microsoft Word. To cope with this, save your work in a different format by selecting e.g. Rich Text Format from the *Save As type* box.

Print Preview

When typing and editing, it is hard to get a feel for the look of the finished piece of work. Check your work before printing as this is the only way to discover that everything is squashed in one corner, or one word has just gone over onto a second page!

To preview work, view the document in Print Preview. Zoom in on details, correct basic spacing errors and then print directly from here or close and return to the Normal view.

To carry out document editing, click off the Magnifier button. A cursor will appear on screen and you can now alter spacing or delete text in the normal way.

Turn magnifier off to edit

2 Set the Zoom level

4 Select the page display

6 Click Close

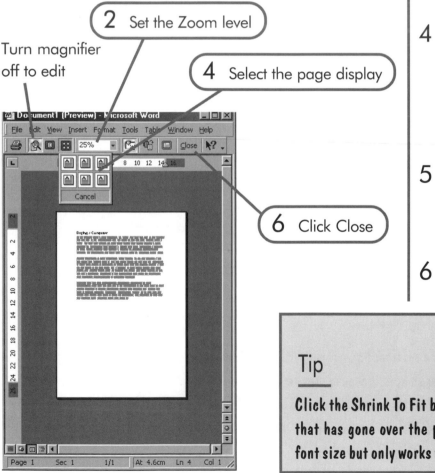

1 Click the Print Preview button or select it from the File menu.

2 Set the magnification by altering the percentage in the Zoom box.

3 Switch between this setting and 100% zoom by clicking on the page when the pointer shows a magnifying glass.

4 Click the Multiple Pages button and select the number of pages to see by clicking and dragging the pointer across the squares.

5 To see the next or previous pages, press the Page Up or Page Down keys.

6 Click Close to return to Normal view.

Tip

Click the Shrink To Fit button 🖺 to pull back text that has gone over the page. This will reduce the font size but only works for a small amount of text.

Basic Steps

1 For one copy of your document, click the Print button 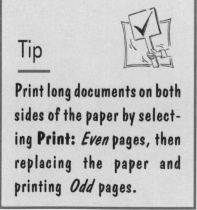.

2 To alter default settings, select File – Page Set up to change paper size or orientation.

3 Select File – Print to open the Print dialog box.

4 Select the printer in the Name slot.

5 Enter the number of copies, and either click Current page or type the page numbers in the Print range Pages slot to specify which pages are printed.

6 Click OK.

Tip

Print long documents on both sides of the paper by selecting Print: *Even* pages, then replacing the paper and printing *Odd* pages.

You can prepare the page for printing via **Page Setup.** The default prints documents on upright A4 (Portrait) and you need to select Landscape Orientation by clicking in the round (radio) button if you want the longer edges top and bottom. You can also select different sized paper on which to print..

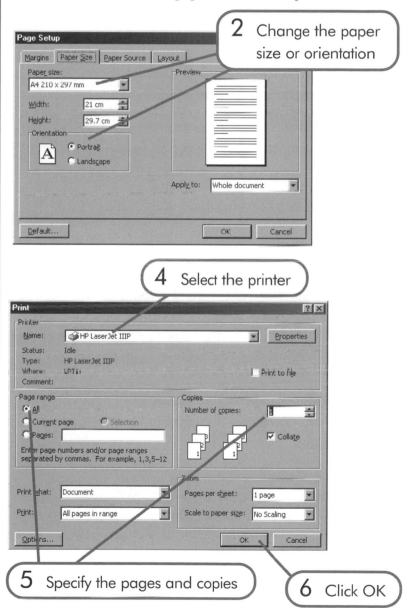

2 Change the paper size or orientation

4 Select the printer

5 Specify the pages and copies

6 Click OK

Summary

- [ ] When entering long sentences, you can leave word wrap to move text onto the next line whenever the right margin is reached. To start new lines or paragraphs, however, you must press [Enter].

- [ ] Correcting spelling and grammar is made easy as Word puts red or green wavy lines under words that need checking.

- [ ] If you make a mistake, the Undo button can put things right by stepping back one action at a time.

- [ ] Help is available in a number of places, particularly from the Help menu and through the Office Assistant.

- [ ] If you first select entries with the mouse or keyboard, you can make changes to the appearance of the text or to line spacing, text alignment and paragraph indentation using the toolbar shortcuts or Format menu options.

- [ ] Saving work is straightforward if you are clear where you want to save it, and what name it should have.

- [ ] It is a good idea to update your work regularly by clicking the Save toolbar button.

- [ ] Before printing, check your document in Print Preview so that you can make final adjustments to spacing and page layout.

4 Extra Word features

Pictures

A quick way to improve the look of your work, or clarify a point, is to add a relevant picture. Although you can use an application such as Paint to create your own pictures, or download wonderful images from the World Wide Web, for most of us its easiest to select from the ready-made gallery known as ClipArt.

A shortcut to the ClipArt gallery is located on the Drawing toolbar, but you can also reach it via the **Insert** menu.

Once you have inserted your picture, you can change its size and position and even alter specific details such as colour and orientation using the drawing tools.

Go back to the
main categories

6   Close the gallery

3   Use key word search

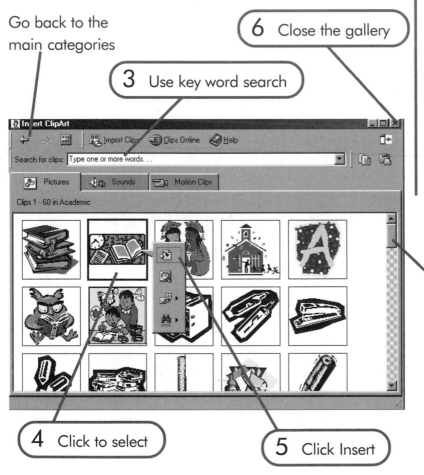

4   Click to select

5   Click Insert

1   Click in position on the screen then click the Insert Clip Art toolbar button or go to Insert - Picture – Clip Art.

2   In the Insert ClipArt dialog box, click a category then scroll through the pictures that appear until you find one you want.

Or

3   Type in key words and press [Enter].

4   Select a picture by clicking it once.

5   Click the Insert button or press Enter.

6   Close the gallery to see the picture underneath.

2   Scroll through the pictures

- ❏ Resizing a picture

1 Click to select it.

2 Move the pointer over a sizing handle where it will show a 2-way arrow and drag the border in or out.

- ❏ Using a text box

3 Go to Insert – Textbox, or click the Text Box button 🖹 on the Drawing toolbar.

4 Click on the screen when the pointer shows a cross. A small box will appear.

5 Insert a picture *inside* the textbox.

6 Select the text box edge – it will show a thick line and *white* sizing handles – and resize or move the picture.

7 Click the Line Color tool to remove the visible text box line or change its colour.

A *selected* picture shows a black border and small boxes – sizing handles – and in this state can be resized. It can also be deleted by pressing the **[Delete]** key, or re-aligned using the alignment toolbar buttons.

To position a picture on the page more exactly, you need to insert it into a *Text Box*.

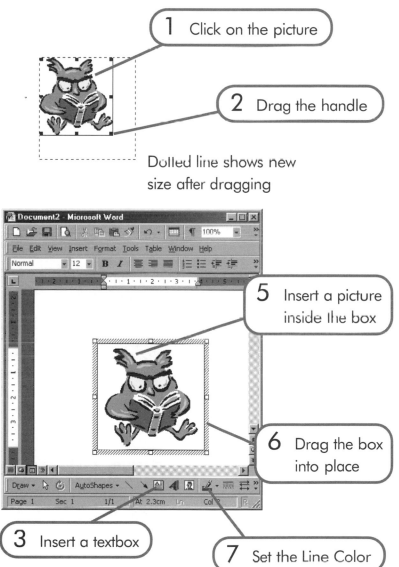

1 Click on the picture

2 Drag the handle

Dotted line shows new size after dragging

5 Insert a picture inside the box

6 Drag the box into place

3 Insert a textbox

7 Set the Line Color

45

Editing a picture

To make more detailed changes to your picture, right-click to open the editing menu. You will now be able to add a border or caption, change the brightness or colour and generally custom-ise the picture in a range of different ways.

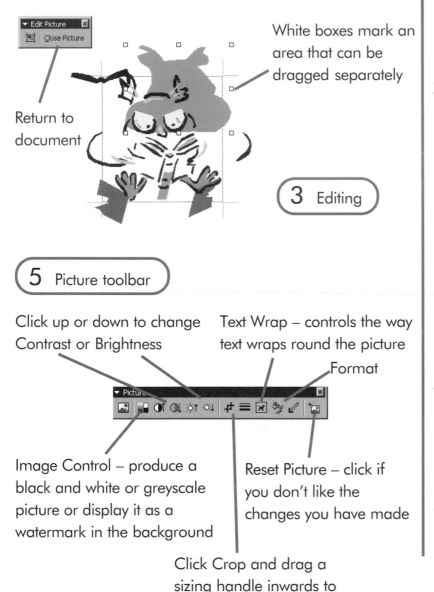

White boxes mark an area that can be dragged separately

Return to document

3 Editing

5 Picture toolbar

Click up or down to change Contrast or Brightness

Text Wrap – controls the way text wraps round the picture

Format

Image Control – produce a black and white or greyscale picture or display it as a watermark in the background

Reset Picture – click if you don't like the changes you have made

Click Crop and drag a sizing handle inwards to remove an unwanted area

1 Right-click the picture to open the short menu.

2 Select Borders and Shading to place a border round the picture, or Caption to add a title.

3 Edit Picture will place the picture on a new page within a frame. Here you can drag individual parts to new positions, or edit parts using the drawing tools (see next page). Return to your document by clicking the Close Picture button or select-ing File – Close and Return to Document.

4 Select Format Picture to make precise changes to measurements or add a background colour.

5 Select Show Picture Toolbar for a further range of shortcuts.

Basic steps

1 If no Drawing Toolbar is visible, select it from the View – Toolbars menu or click on the Drawing button.

2 Select a free line, rectangle, oval or other AutoShape from the toolbar then move the pointer on the screen. It will show a cross.

3 Click and drag the cross across the page to create the shape.

Drawings

When you want to add arrows, squares or freestyle drawings of your own, you can use the range of drawing tools available within Word.

Once you have drawn a basic shape, you can fill it with colour, rotate or flip it or select several shapes and group them into one.

Apart from the more commonly used lines, arrows and geometric shapes, you can add Callouts as 'speech bubbles', or WordArt text in bendy shapes. You can also box text and make it stand out with colours, shadows or 3-D effects.

Drawing Toolbar

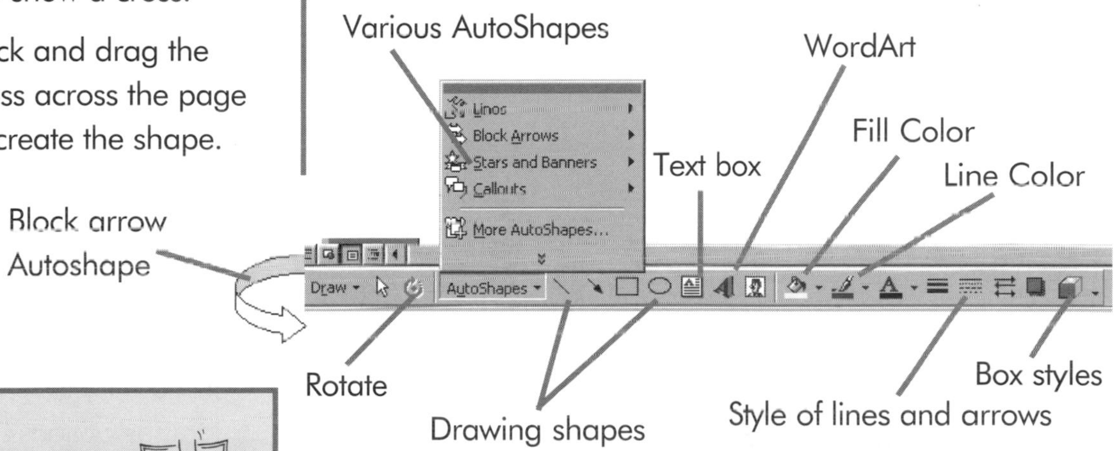

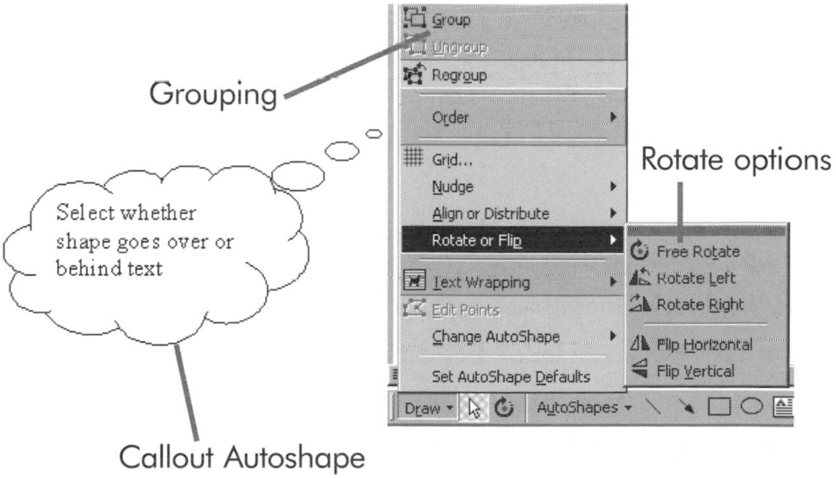

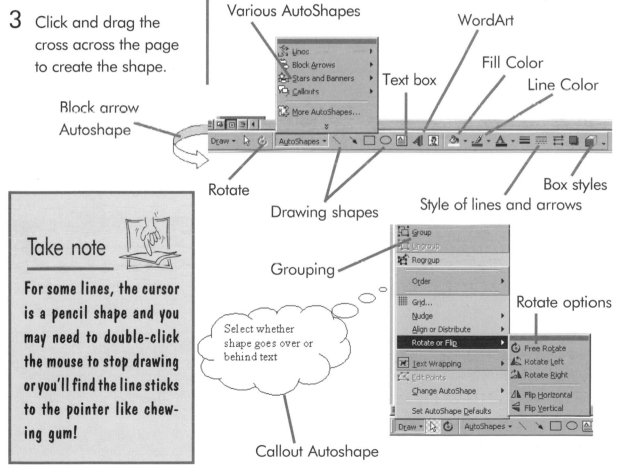

Take note

For some lines, the cursor is a pencil shape and you may need to double-click the mouse to stop drawing or you'll find the line sticks to the pointer like chewing gum!

Basic steps

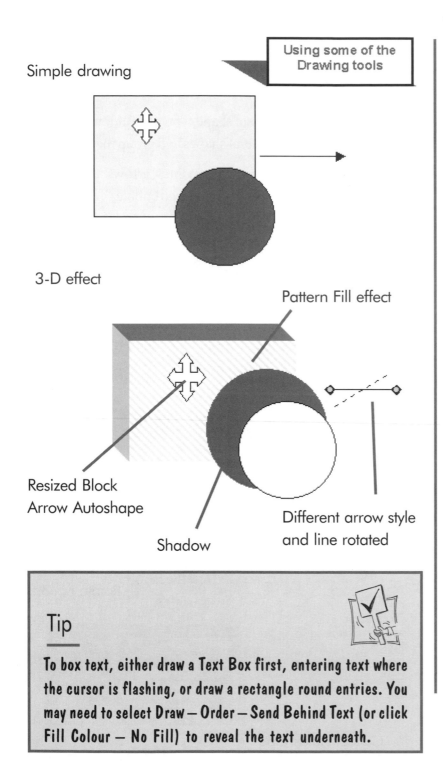

Simple drawing

3-D effect

Pattern Fill effect

Resized Block
Arrow Autoshape

Shadow

Different arrow style
and line rotated

Using some of the Drawing tools

❑ Editing a shape

1 Click to show the white sizing handles.

2 Drag any sizing handle with the 2-way arrow to increase or decrease the size of the shape. On a callout, you can drag a yellow triangle appearing at its tip to change its position on the marked object.

3 When the mouse pointer shows a 4-way arrow, click on the drawn object to drag it around the screen.

4 Change the line style or fill colour using the toolbar options.

5 To rotate a shape, click the Rotate button on the toolbar. Green circles will replace the sizing handles and any of these can be dragged to a new position.

Tip

To box text, either draw a Text Box first, entering text where the cursor is flashing, or draw a rectangle round entries. You may need to select Draw – Order – Send Behind Text (or click Fill Colour – No Fill) to reveal the text underneath.

Borders and shading

1 Select the text and go to Format – Borders and Shading…

2 On the Borders tab, select the type of border, the line thickness and style, and check that these are applied to the correct section.

❑ If you change your mind, remove the border by selecting *None* as the Setting.

3 On the Shading tab you can add coloured or patterned backgrounds to the box.

4 Select Page Border to edge the page with lines or pictures.

5 Click OK to return to your document.

You can create attractive boxes of text by bordering and shading parts of a document, and you can also border a whole page. The options are in the **Format – Borders and Shading** dialog box.

When text borders appear, they often apply to the entire paragraph. Select the text and then click **Apply to Text** if you want the border to fit just the text entry.

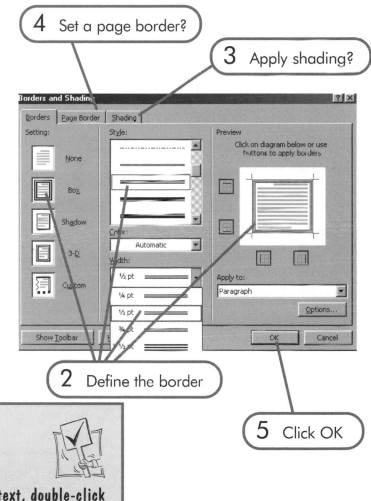

4 Set a page border?

3 Apply shading?

2 Define the border

5 Click OK

Tip

To continue work below bordered text, double-click the cursor in position. Don't press [Enter] or you will extend the border into the new paragraph.

Margins

Every new document has a left, right, top and bottom margin where text is not normally typed. The default settings are:

    Top and Bottom 1" (2.54cm)

    Left and Right 1.5" (3.17cm)

For some documents, these white spaces may be too wide or too narrow and you will want to change them. You can either change the measurements exactly, or do it roughly by eye using the Ruler.

Basic steps

❏ Using the Ruler

1 Select View – Print Layout to show the margins clearly.

2 Move the mouse pointer between the white and grey areas on the ruler until it changes to a two-way arrow.

3 Click and hold the button and a dotted line will appear down the page.

4 Drag the line in the appropriate direction to increase or decrease the margin.

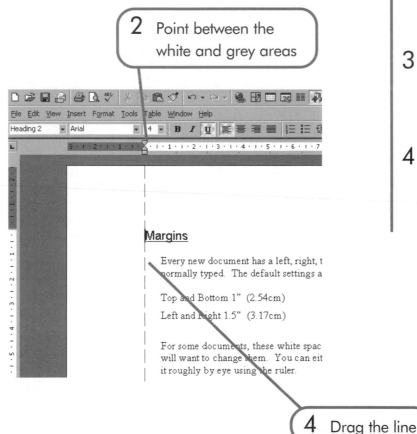

2 Point between the white and grey areas

4 Drag the line

Basic steps

1 In the File – Page Set up dialog box, click the Margins tab.

2 For any margin, move the measurement up or down in 10ths by clicking the arrow.

Or

3 Type in new measure-ments – you do not need to add the units.

4 Set the Apply to option – the whole document, the section or from the current point forward.

5 Preview the changes before clicking OK.

6 If you want to use the new measurements regularly, click Default to set them for all new documents.

Using the dialog box

To alter margins exactly, click the Margin tab in the **File – Page Set up** dialog box and then change the measurements showing in the relevant boxes. Unlike paragraph formatting, you don't need to select any part of the document first unless you want the margin change restricted.

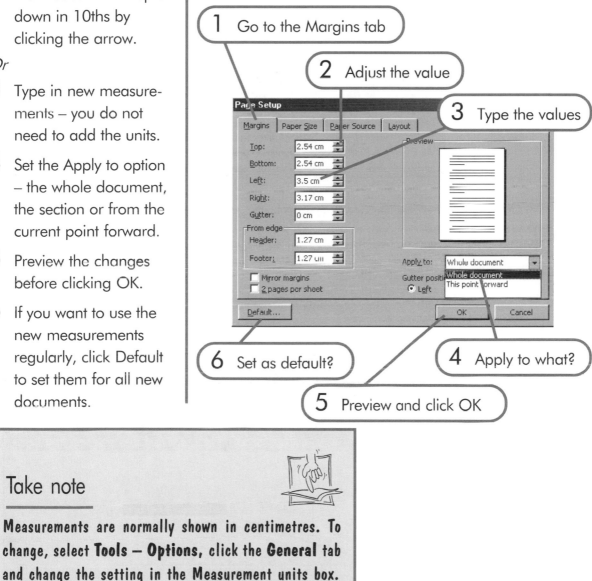

1 Go to the Margins tab

2 Adjust the value

3 Type the values

6 Set as default?

4 Apply to what?

5 Preview and click OK

Take note

Measurements are normally shown in centimetres. To change, select **Tools – Options**, click the **General** tab and change the setting in the **Measurement units** box.

Moving and copying text

It often happens that words, paragraphs or other items such as pictures need to be moved or copied to a different part of the document. To save retyping, you can use two different techniques commonly known as *drag and drop* and *cut and paste*.

Drag and drop

Dragging selected text with the mouse is best for moving single words or paragraphs short distances on the visible part of the screen. After dragging, text may take on the alignment of the closest entries, but this can be sorted out quite easily.

1 Select the text.

2 Move the pointer over the block until it shows a white arrow. Hold down the button. A small box will appear at the end of the arrow.

3 Drag the arrow to the new position for the text. A vertical dotted line will move with it.

4 Release the mouse button and the text will drop into place.

❑ To copy, but not move, the text, hold down [Control] as you drag. A cross will appear below the box.

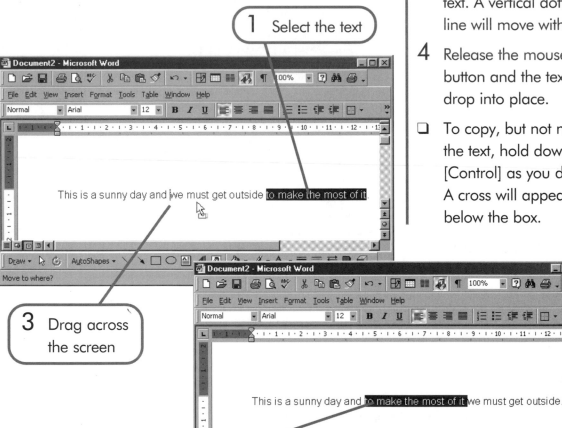

1 Select the text

3 Drag across the screen

4 Drop into place

Basic steps

1 Select the text.

2 Use a toolbar button, or select the Edit menu, or right-click on the text and pick from the short menu: Cut ✂ to move, Copy 📋 for a copy.

3 Click in the new position for the text.

4 Click Paste 📋 or select Edit – Paste.

Cut and Paste

To move larger blocks of text over longer distances, perhaps across pages or to another document or application altogether, it is best to use Cut/Copy and Paste.

To leave the original in place, a **copy** of the selected text is placed in a temporary part of the computer's memory known as the Clipboard. To move text, you must **cut** it out of the document before placing it in the Clipboard. When ready, text from the Clipboard is **pasted** into its new position.

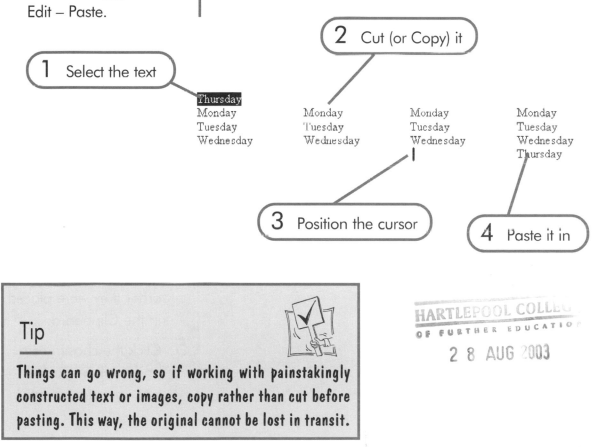

Tip

Things can go wrong, so if working with painstakingly constructed text or images, copy rather than cut before pasting. This way, the original cannot be lost in transit.

The Clipboard in Word 2000

Earlier versions of Word only allowed one item at a time to be held in the Clipboard, but now it can store up to 12 different entries at once. This means that you can transfer a number of entries across pages, documents or even applications. However, when pasting, you need to check that the correct text or pictures will appear in your document.

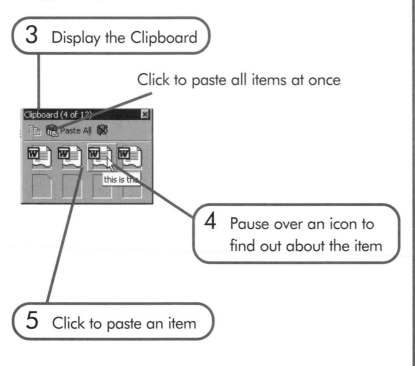

3   Display the Clipboard

Click to paste all items at once

Clipboard (4 of 12)

Paste All

this is th

4   Pause over an icon to find out about the item

5   Click to paste an item

1 Cut or copy items as normal.

2 If you want to paste the last item cut or copied, then Paste as normal.

3 If you have cut or copied more than one item, the Clipboard toolbar may appear automatically. If not, show it by selecting View – Toolbars – Clipboard. Each item will be displayed as an icon in a separate slot.

4 To choose an item, rest your mouse on any icon. The first few words of text entries will appear, although pictures may only be labelled Item 1, Item 2 etc., depending on the order they were placed in the Clipboard.

5 Click the chosen item and it will be pasted into your document.

Find or replace text

1 Select Edit – Replace.

2 Enter the original text in the Find What box *exactly* as it appears in the document.

3 Enter the new text in the Replace With box.

4 Click Find Next. The first matching text will be highlighted in your document.

5 Click Replace, or Find Next to skip to the next match.

❑ To find text

6 Select Edit – Find or click and complete the boxes as above.

7 Click Find Next to locate the first matching entry.

A useful shortcut offered by Word when working with longer documents is to find and replace text or punctuation automatically, or go directly to a particular page. You could, for example, use an abbreviation throughout a document and replace all such entries with the full text that only needs to be typed once, or find a reference to a particular word without searching every page.

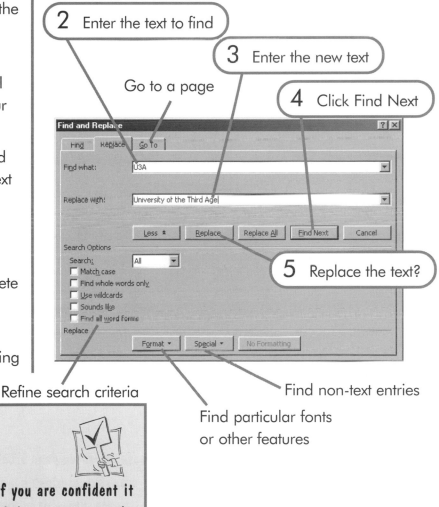

2 Enter the text to find

3 Enter the new text

Go to a page

4 Click Find Next

5 Replace the text?

Refine search criteria

Find particular fonts or other features

Find non-text entries

Tip

Only click Replace All if you are confident it will be straightforward. Otherwise, you might replace parts of words you wanted to retain.

Starting a new page

As you type a long document, a new page starts automatically when you reach the bottom of the screen. However, this point will change as you add or delete text or images.

If you always want an entry to start on a new page, perhaps a fresh chapter or the first piece of text following a title page, you need to produce a 'hard break' in your document. This will then be retained whatever happens to the rest of your work.

To see the break, click the Show/Hide button that reveals all keyboard strokes and you will see it represented as follows:

...............................Page Break......................................

Basic steps

1 Click the cursor in the position for the break.

2 Use the keyboard shortcut: [Control] plus [Enter].

Or

3 Open the Insert menu and select Break...

4 Check the Page break option is selected.

5 Click OK.

6 To delete the break, click on the dotted line and press [Delete].

3 Use Insert – Break...

Insert
- Break...
- Page Numbers...
- Date and Time...
- Symbol...
- Caption...
- Picture ▶
- File...
- Object...

Break [?][X]

Break types
- ● Page break
- ○ Column break
- ○ Text wrapping break

Section break types
- ○ Next page
- ○ Continuous
- ○ Even page
- ○ Odd page

[OK]   [Cancel]

4 Select Page break

5 Click OK

Tip

You can sometimes create unwanted page breaks by accident, which will spread your document over several blank pages. To delete these, move to the end page and click the Show/Hide button. Now delete all the Enter symbols ¶ until you find yourself back on the last page of text.

Basic steps

1 Select Insert – Page Numbers to open the dialog box.

2 Choose where the numbers should go.

3 Click Format...

4 Change the style (e.g. a, b, c or i, ii, iii, etc.) or start numbering other than from page 1, as required, and click OK.

5 Check the preview and click OK.

You can choose to omit numbers on the first page of a document

Rather than number each page manually, which would mean amending numbers as you add extra pages of typing, Word will insert page numbers into the top or bottom margin and update them automatically.

You can include page numbers within a header or footer (see page 61) or insert them from the **Insert** menu.

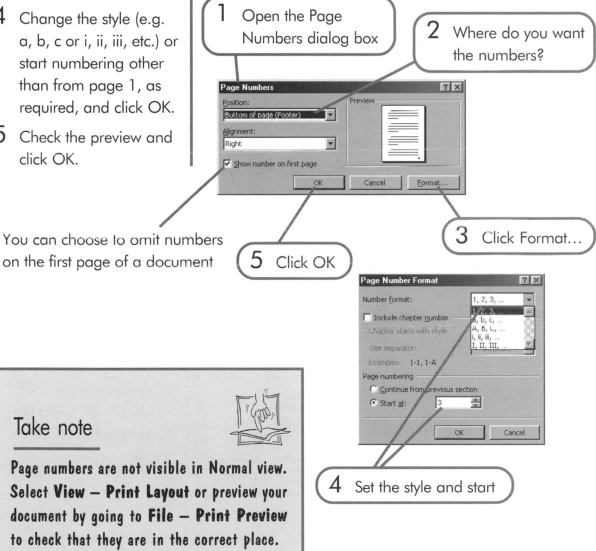

1 Open the Page Numbers dialog box

2 Where do you want the numbers?

3 Click Format...

5 Click OK

4 Set the style and start

Take note

Page numbers are not visible in Normal view. Select **View – Print Layout** or preview your document by going to **File – Print Preview** to check that they are in the correct place.

Symbols and dates

To enter a character not available on the keyboard, you can select a symbol from the range available in the Symbol box. You can also save time entering the date by selecting it from the **Insert** menu.

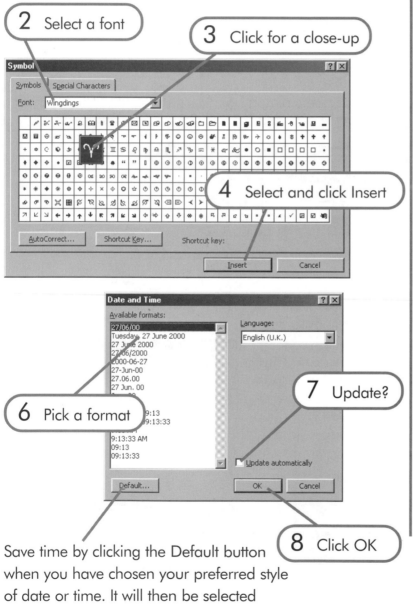

2 Select a font

3 Click for a close-up

4 Select and click Insert

6 Pick a format

7 Update?

8 Click OK

Save time by clicking the Default button when you have chosen your preferred style of date or time. It will then be selected whenever you open the dialog box.

❑ Inserting symbols

1 Click in position for the symbol in your document, and then go to Insert – Symbol.

2 Scroll through the fonts to view the sets.

3 Click on a character to see it in close-up.

4 When you find the symbol you want, select it, click Insert then click Close to return to your document.

❑ Inserting the date

5 Select Insert – Date and Time.

6 Select your preferred format and click OK.

7 If you will be delaying printing but want the current date in your document, select Update automatically.

8 Click OK.

Basic steps

❑ Previously saved object

1 Select Insert – Object and click the Create from File tab.

2 In the dialog box, type in the file name, or click Browse to locate the file – the name will be inserted into the File name box.

3 If you click Link to file, changes made to the original will be reflected in the Word document.

4 Select Display as icon if you want to save space.

5 Click OK to import the file into your document.

6 Double-click the object to go to the original application for editing.

You can use any of the applications installed on your computer to create a new object such as a chart, spreadsheet or picture within your document, or locate and import one that was previously created elsewhere.

When you double-click the imported object, you can use the specialised toolbars and menu options available in the original application to make any changes.

You can also choose to insert just an icon representing the object, which you must then double-click to view.

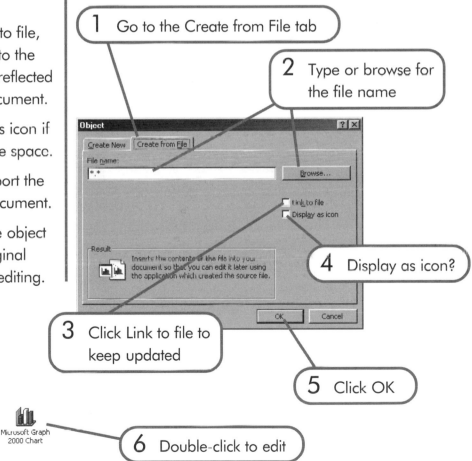

1 Go to the Create from File tab

2 Type or browse for the file name

3 Click Link to file to keep updated

4 Display as icon?

5 Click OK

6 Double-click to edit

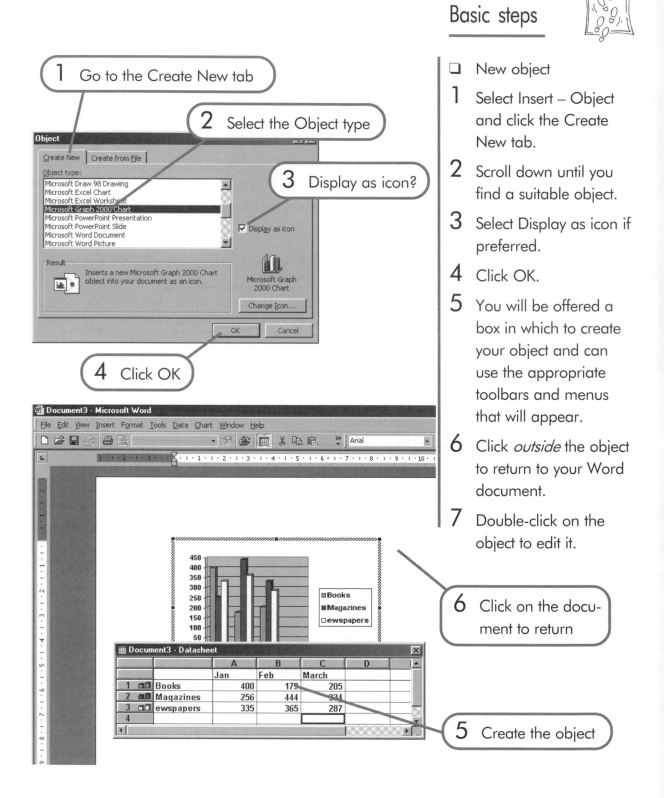

1 Go to the Create New tab

2 Select the Object type

3 Display as icon?

Object

Create New | Create from File

Object type:

Microsoft Draw 98 Drawing
Microsoft Excel Chart
Microsoft Excel Worksheet
Microsoft Graph 2000 Chart
Microsoft PowerPoint Presentation
Microsoft PowerPoint Slide
Microsoft Word Document
Microsoft Word Picture

☑ Display as icon

Microsoft Graph
2000 Chart

Result
Inserts a new Microsoft Graph 2000 Chart object into your document as an icon.

Change Icon...

OK | Cancel

4 Click OK

Document3 - Microsoft Word

File Edit View Insert Format Tools Data Chart Window Help

Arial

	Jan	Feb	March	D
1 Books	400	179	205	
2 Magazines	256	444	334	
3 ewspapers	335	365	287	
4				

Document3 - Datasheet

6 Click on the document to return

5 Create the object

❑ New object

1 Select Insert – Object and click the Create New tab.

2 Scroll down until you find a suitable object.

3 Select Display as icon if preferred.

4 Click OK.

5 You will be offered a box in which to create your object and can use the appropriate toolbars and menus that will appear.

6 Click *outside* the object to return to your Word document.

7 Double-click on the object to edit it.

Headers and footers

1 Select View – Headers and Footers

2 For a header, enter your text in the box, formatting it as normal. Realign the cursor using [Tab].

3 Use the toolbar to insert page numbers, dates or times.

4 To set different headers within a document, go to Page Set up – Layout.

5 To go to the footer box, click the Switch Be- lween Header and Footer button.

6 Close the toolbar and check in Print Layout view (where header text is shown in grey).

7 To delete headers or footers, double-click the entry or select View – Headers and Footers and switch to the rel- evant box. Ensure text is fully selected before pressing [Delete].

If you want the same text at the top or bottom of every page, e.g. a company logo or the title of your report, you can insert entries in the margins as headers or footers. This way, they don't affect the layout of your work and you can even have different entries on the front or alternate pages.

When you are creating headers or footers, the text of your document is shown in grey. Switch between views by double-clicking the text in the header box or in your main document.

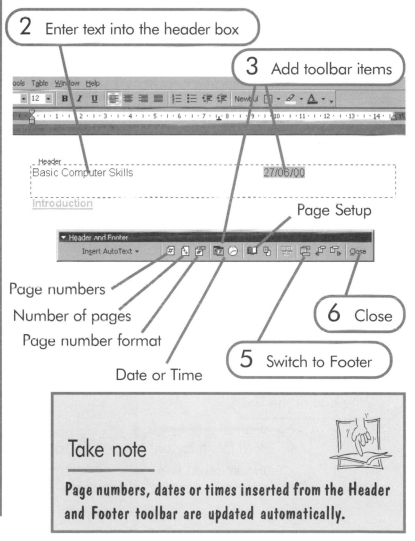

2 Enter text into the header box

3 Add toolbar items

Page Setup

Page numbers

Number of pages

Page number format

Date or Time

6 Close

5 Switch to Footer

Take note

Page numbers, dates or times inserted from the Header and Footer toolbar are updated automatically.

Creating lists

Whenever you have a list of entries that need to be numbered, you can either set numbering before you type, or add the numbers later. In the same way, you can emphasise points with bullets. Once numbers or bullets have been set, they are added automatically when you press **[Enter]** and start a new line.

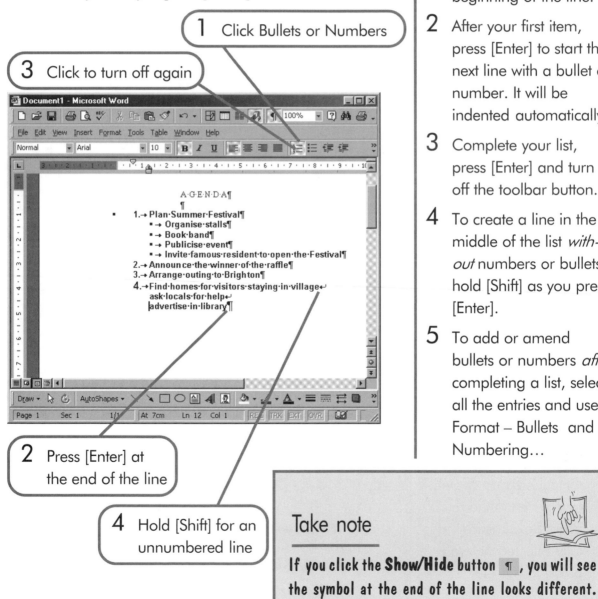

1 Click Bullets or Numbers

3 Click to turn off again

2 Press [Enter] at the end of the line

4 Hold [Shift] for an unnumbered line

Take note

If you click the **Show/Hide** button ¶ , you will see the symbol at the end of the line looks different.

Basic steps

1 To change number or bullet attributes, open the Format – Bullets and Numbering dialog box.

2 Select the appropriate tab.

3 Click on a style.

4 If you break off a list, e.g. to insert a drawing, select the Restart or Continue option if necessary.

5 Click OK.

❑ Customizing

6 To customise styles, or alter the spacing between numbers or bullets and list items, click Customize…

7 Define the style and click OK.

Formatting bullets and numbers

The toolbar buttons are easy to use, but go to the **Format – Bullets and Numbering** menu to amend styles or spacing.

1 Open the Bullets and Numbering dialog box

2 Open the tab

Bullets and Numbering

Bulleted | Numbered | Outline Numbered

None

3 Select a style

List numbering

Restart numbering   Continue previous list   Customize…

Reset   OK   Cancel

4 Restart or Continue?

6 Click Customize…

5 Click OK

7 Define the style

Customize Numbered List

Number format

Font…   OK   Cancel

Number style: a, b, c, …   Start at: d

Number position

Left   Aligned at: 0.63 cm

Text position

Indent at: 1.27 cm

Preview

d
e
f

Tables

To create neat columns of text or numbers in your work, you can insert a table and enter your data into the squares – *cells* - that appear. Each cell is independent and so entries can be aligned or formatted differently within each one.

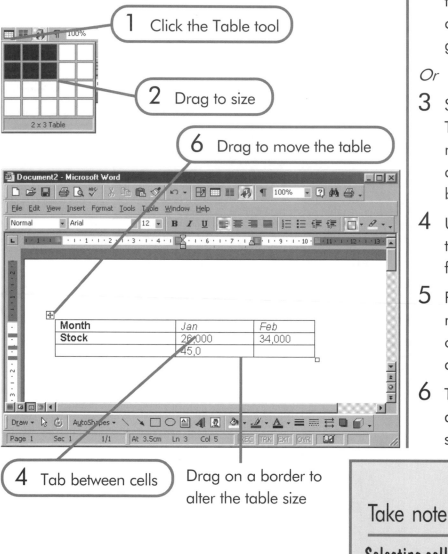

1 Click the Table tool

2 Drag to size

6 Drag to move the table

4 Tab between cells

Drag on a border to alter the table size

1 Position the cursor then click ▦ the Table tool.

2 Drag the mouse across the required number of cells and, when you let go a table will appear.

Or

3 Select Table – Insert Table, enter the number of rows and columns in the dialog box and click OK.

4 Use [Tab] or the mouse to move between cells for text entry.

5 Press [Enter] to create a new line within the cell, or let word wrap fill the cell with a long entry.

6 To move the table, click and drag the small selection box.

Take note

Selecting cells and pressing [Delete] will only remove cell entries and will **NOT** remove entire columns or rows.

Basic steps

☐ Inserting and deleting

1 Click in the last cell and press [Tab] to add a new row.

Or

2 Select any cell and add a column or row by going to Table – Insert and choosing a Row or Column option.

3 To delete a column or row, select it then use Table – Delete and click a delete option.

☐ Enhancing

4 Format selected cells or the table via the Borders and Shading dialog box (page 49).

5 To remove borders, set Settings to *None*.

Or

6 For colours or shading use the borders and backgrounds options on the Tables and Borders toolbar.

Amending columns and rows

You will probably find that you need to change the width or height of your table to accommodate entries, and add or delete extra rows or columns once you start entering your data.

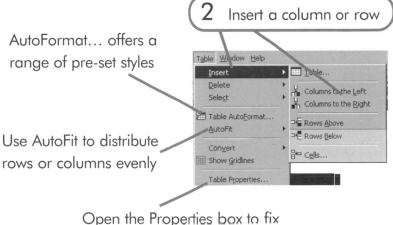

2 Insert a column or row

AutoFormat... offers a range of pre-set styles

Use AutoFit to distribute rows or columns evenly

Open the Properties box to fix row or column sizes accurately

Improving the appearance of a table

Cell borders can be removed before printing to leave simple columns, or retained and emphasised to print data out as a grid.

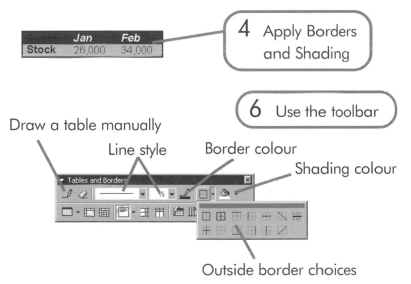

4 Apply Borders and Shading

6 Use the toolbar

Draw a table manually

Line style

Border colour

Shading colour

Outside border choices

Mail merge

It is always pleasanter to receive a personalised letter or invitation than one addressed to 'Dear Sir/Madam'. In order to save time when sending out such documents, you can build up a database of details for everyone on your mailing list and add the appropriate information to each letter automatically.

There are two files that need to be created for a mail merge:

● The letter, invitation, demand, etc. that forms the **Main Document**;

● Names, addresses and other details that form the **Data Source**.

By following the steps set out in the Mail Merge Helper dialog box, you can create and edit your files in the correct order.

Basic steps

❑ Create Main Document

1 Wherever you are in Word, select Tools – Mail Merge.

2 In Step 1 click Main Document – Create.

3 Select Form Letters... to create any main document other than labels or envelopes.

4 In the new window that appears, click Active Window to use the document you are working on, or start a New Main Document.

5 *Don't* select Edit Main Document yet, but move on to Step 2 so that you can first set up your database.

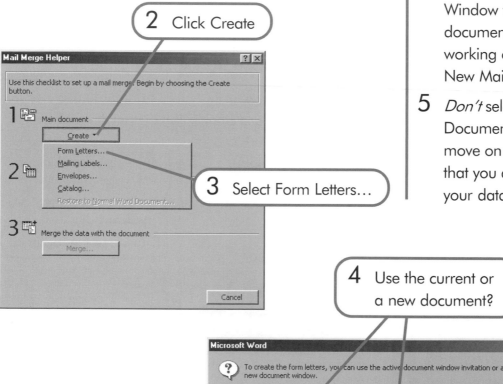

2 Click Create

3 Select Form Letters...

4 Use the current or a new document?

Creating the Data Source

1 Click Data Source –
Get Data – Create
Data Source (or Open
to use an existing
database).

2 In the Create Data
Source dialog box,
remove any unwanted
fields by selecting them
and clicking Remove
Field Name.

3 Add fields if required
by typing in the Field
Name and clicking Add
Field Name.

4 When you have all field
names listed, click OK
and save the file.

5 Select Edit Data Source
to open the Data Form
and enter details of the
first person (forming
Record 1) on the mail-
ing list. Use [Tab] to
move between boxes.

6 Click Add New to move
to Record 2.

7 ONLY when all records
have been entered,
click OK.

You will be offered a standard list of categories (known as
fields) for your mailing list e.g. first name, surname, town, etc.
After amending the field names, use the Data Form to enter
details of everyone on your mailing list into the Data Source.

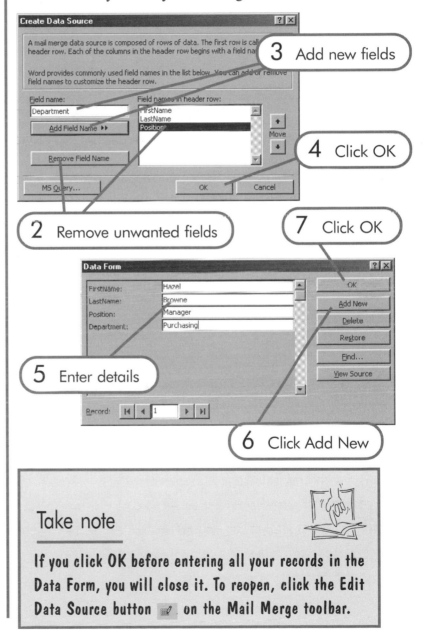

3 Add new fields

4 Click OK

2 Remove unwanted fields

7 Click OK

5 Enter details

6 Click Add New

Take note

If you click OK before entering all your records in the
Data Form, you will close it. To reopen, click the Edit
Data Source button 📝 on the Mail Merge toolbar.

Merging documents

When you have entered all the records into your database, you'll return to your Main Document where a new toolbar appears – the Mail Merge toolbar.

Now you can start completing your Main Document. Don't type everyone's details, but insert the relevant field name instead. This appears between <<chevrons>> against a shaded background and, when you print your letters, the correct details from each record will be drawn from the database.

The **View Merged Data** button lets you check what these finished letters will look like with the data inserted into the fields.

When your document is complete, the choices now are to save the main document and data source separately – although the link will be maintained when you open the main document again - to print all the merged letters, or to save them in a separate merged file for printing another day.

Tip

To print a limited selection of documents, click the Mail Merge Helper button 🖼 and, in Step **3**, select Merge. You can now choose which records to include.

1 Create your document as before but instead of typing details, e.g. after *Dear,* select a field name from the Insert Merge Field drop-down list. The field name will appear.

2 Press the [Space Bar] or [Enter] and continue typing and inserting field names until your document is complete.

3 Click the View Merged Data button to see the first record.

4 Click the Next Record button to see the next.

5 Click View Merged Data again to return to the Main Document.

6 Click Merge to New Document to save the merged documents in a separate file.

7 Click Merge to Printer to print the documents.

8 Save and close the Main Document and the Data Source file.

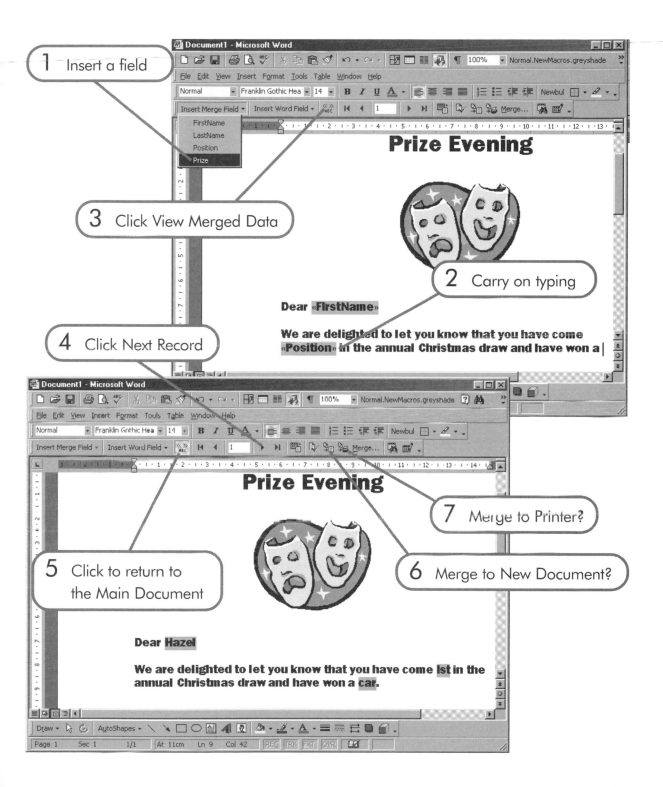

1 Insert a field

3 Click View Merged Data

2 Carry on typing

4 Click Next Record

5 Click to return to the Main Document

7 Merge to Printer?

6 Merge to New Document?

Summary

❑ Your own drawings, or pictures from the Clip Art gallery, can be inserted into documents and then moved, re-sized or otherwise altered using the editing and formatting tools.

❑ Another way to enhance text is to add a border or shade the background.

❑ When you want to copy or re-position any entries, you can drag them to new places or copy them over and over again using the Paste option.

❑ Margins can be altered by eye or by an exact figure entered in the margin measurement boxes.

❑ If you need a special symbol, or a chart or drawing produced elsewhere, you can add or link it to your document.

❑ You can also add page numbers and dates that will update automatically over time, and include the same entries on every page by creating headers or footers.

❑ Lists can be numbered or enhanced with bullets, and the style and spacing can be customised to your liking.

❑ To save time sending the same letter to a number of people, you can type it once and then personalise it by merging it with data held in a separately created database.

5 Spreadsheets

The right address

Spreadsheets allow you to present numerical data and perform calculations. They can be particularly useful at home if you want to keep an eye on your finances, work out quantities for DIY or cooking, keep scores in games or compare prices.

When you open Microsoft Excel from the icon ___| or **Start** – **Programs** menu, the first sheet of your workbook opens directly on screen. You can make entries on any sheet by clicking the sheet tab at the bottom of the screen, and all sheets will be saved automatically when you save the file.

Each sheet looks like squared paper and each square is known as a *cell*. At the head of each column of cells is a letter, and there is a number at the start of each row. So that you can refer to a particular cell on the sheet, each cell is known by its column and row e.g. A2 or B3. This is the *cell address*.

Moving around

- ❑ To go to a cell, use any of these methods:

  Click into the cell

  Press [Tab] to move a column to the right

  Hold [Shift] as you press [Tab] to move to the left

  Press [Enter] to move down the column

  Press an arrow key to move in that direction

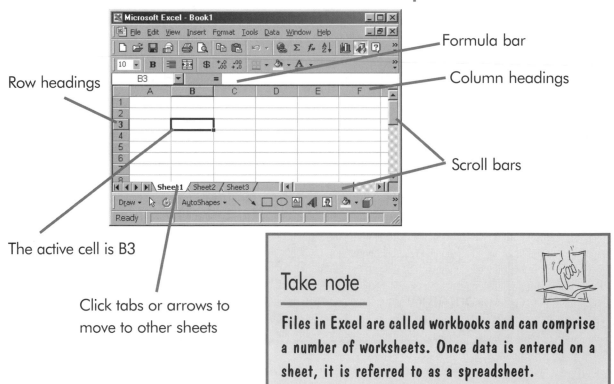

Row headings

Formula bar

Column headings

Scroll bars

The active cell is B3

Click tabs or arrows to move to other sheets

Take note

Files in Excel are called workbooks and can comprise a number of worksheets. Once data is entered on a sheet, it is referred to as a spreadsheet.

Basic steps

❑ Selecting cells

1 Click or move to any cell. It will show a darker border and is known as the active cell. (A1 is automatically selected at first.)

2 To select more than one cell at a time, move the pointer over the first cell in the range. It will show a fat white cross ⬚.

3 Click and drag the cross down the column or along the row. Adjacent cells will now all be selected.

4 After making changes to the selected cells, click anywhere on the sheet to remove the highlight.

5 To select non-adjacent rows or columns, select the first block of cells, then hold down [Control] as you select further blocks.

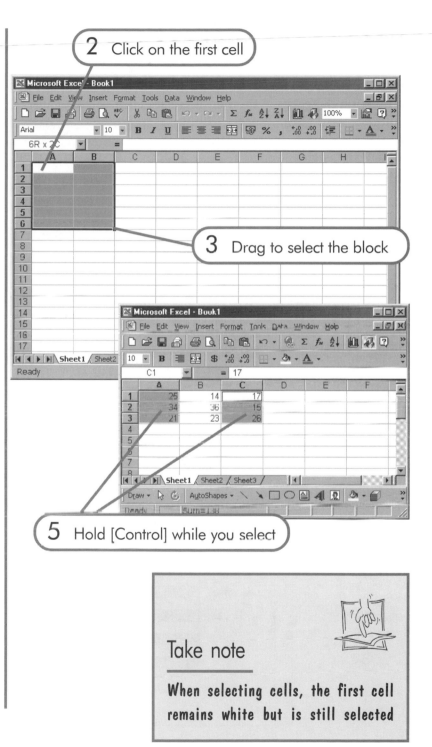

2 Click on the first cell

3 Drag to select the block

5 Hold [Control] while you select

Take note

When selecting cells, the first cell remains white but is still selected

Creating a spreadsheet

As you type, entries will appear in both the active cell and in the Formula bar. To amend an entry, you have three choices: double click the cell; select it and press [F2] to place the cursor inside; or click on the entry in the Formula bar. Then delete or insert entries as you would when word-processing.

So that the spreadsheet is easy to understand, you can widen columns, re-format headings and border or shade particular sections. You can then print the results as a spreadsheet or use the data to create a chart.

1   Open Excel and move to the first cell for data entry.

2   Enter text, symbols or numbers into the active cell.

3   Move down columns or across rows to enter data in different cells.

4   Amend cell entries if you make a mistake or want to reformat entries – full details on the following pages.

5   Save the workbook by clicking the Save button and entering its name and location in the Save As dialog box.

Address of active cell

Formula bar showing formula

	A	B	C	D
	D4	▼	=	=C4/B4*100
1		**Cat Food Prices**		
2	Brand	Size of can (gms)	Cost per can	Cost per 100 gms
3	Kitty	400	£0.55	£0.14
4	Tomcat	1500	£1.56	£0.10
5	Tibbles	700	£0.85	£0.12
6	Bettermeat	400	£0.43	£0.11
7	Morsels	150	£0.25	£0.17
8	AVERAGE	630	£0.73	£0.13
9				

Spreadsheet

Active cell showing answer

Chart

Basic steps

1 Click in the cell where you want the answer to appear.

2 Type the formula, starting with '=' and using operators, cell addresses and values.

3 Press [Enter] or click the ✓ on the Formula bar.

4 Check that the answer is as expected.

5 If it looks incorrect, check your formula in the Formula bar and correct as necessary.

Tip

Instead of *typing* a cell address, you can click on it and its address will be entered into your formula.

Calculations

The joy of Excel is that it will perform calculations for you – but you do have to give it the right instructions. To add the numbers in column A and put a total in A4, you need to write the correct formula. This can use the actual numbers, or the cell addresses.

● For any formula you first enter = to tell Excel to perform a calculation.

● You could now enter the numbers and operators
e.g. =15+14+18

● Use addresses, rather than numbers, so that if you alter the cell contents later, the total is updated automatically
e.g. =A1+A2+A3

This is because the instruction is 'add the contents A1, A2 and A3'. If the contents change, the total will change.

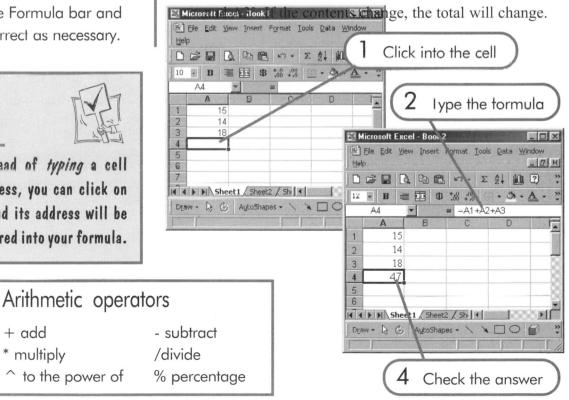

1 Click into the cell

2 Type the formula

4 Check the answer

Arithmetic operators

+ add	- subtract
* multiply	/divide
^ to the power of	% percentage

Useful formulae

For simple calculations, you can use actual figures or cell addresses and simply enter the correct data and operators before pressing [Enter]

$$= A15/7.5$$

When a large number of cells are involved, it can be tedious to enter all the details into a formula. Instead, you can make use of one of the automatic *functions* available in Excel that offer pre-defined formulae structured to perform calculations.

For more complex calculations, help is available via the Paste Function Wizard f_x , but you are most likely to use SUM to total the contents of a range of cells, and AVERAGE to calculate averages. There is a shortcut to the Sum function – the AutoSum.

☐ To use a function

1 Type the = sign then the name of the function (upper or lower case) and an opening bracket e.g. =SUM(

2 Enter the cell range by typing the first cell, then a colon and then the last cell e.g. C4:C8

Or

3 Click the first cell and drag down to the last to enter the range into the formula.

4 Press [Enter] – there is no need to enter the closing bracket first.

☐ AutoSum

5 Select the range of cells.

6 Click the AutoSum button Σ.

The total will appear in the next available cell

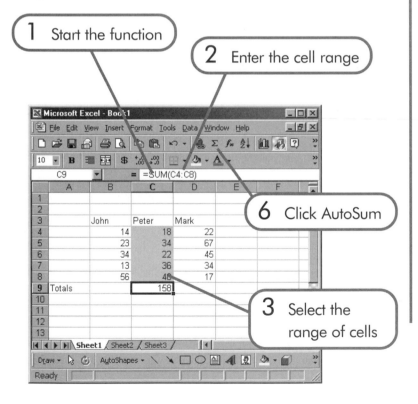

1 Start the function

2 Enter the cell range

6 Click AutoSum

3 Select the range of cells

Basic steps

1 Select the cell(s) you want to change.

2 Click the appropriate toolbar shortcut or go to Format – Cells.

3 Select the Font tab to change the text style, type or size.

4 Preview the changes and then click OK.

Once you have entered text into a cell, you can make various changes to its appearance. Here are some examples:

Regular text (left aligned in cell)
Bold text
Italic text
<u>Underlined text</u>
Right aligned text
Centred text
DIFFERENT FONT TYPE
Different font size

Formatting toolbar

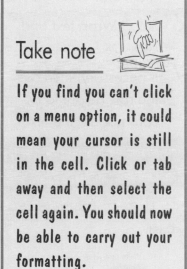

Take note

If you find you can't click on a menu option, it could mean your cursor is still in the cell. Click or tab away and then select the cell again. You should now be able to carry out your formatting.

Format dialog box, Font tab

Click to change orientation or alignment

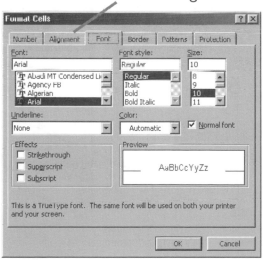

Improving headings

You can improve the appearance of header text in two different ways. Centre a heading with the Merge cells facility, or keep columns narrow by 'wrapping' the heading text.

Basic steps

❑ Centre a heading

1 Type the heading text in the first cell, e.g. A1

2 Select the range of cells across the width of your data, e.g. A1:F1.

3 Click the Merge and Center toolbar button.

❑ Using wrap text

4 Type the heading.

5 Select Format – Cells and click the Alignment tab.

6 Select Wrap text and click OK.

7 If necessary, increase the row height to accommodate the text.

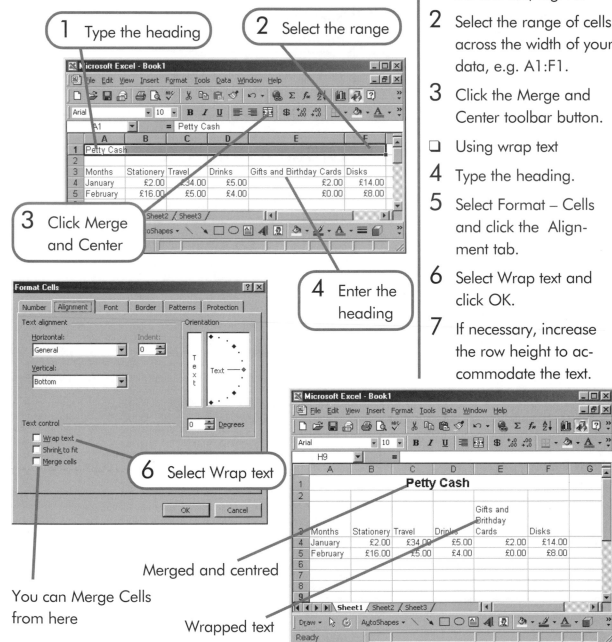

1 Type the heading

2 Select the range

3 Click Merge and Center

4 Enter the heading

6 Select Wrap text

You can Merge Cells from here

Merged and centred

Wrapped text

78

Basic steps

1 Select the cell(s) to be formatted.

2 Click the appropriate toolbar button.

Or

3 Use Format – Cells and go to the Number tab.

4 Select the Category, and amend the Decimal places or Symbol if relevant.

5 Check the sample to make sure formatting is correct and click OK.

❑ To retain numbers starting with 0, e.g. telephone or stock code numbers, format as *Text* or type an apostrophe before the number e.g. '020 7...

Tip

If you find '$' inserted instead of '£', go to **Format – Style – Modify** and select the UK symbol from the list.

Numbers

You can change what you see on screen without changing the underlying *value* of any numeric entry made into a cell by formatting the numbers.

The default setting is *General* so that the cell will display the exact entry. Alternative ways to show the same number, e.g. 7.66 include:

8	*Number* with no decimals, i.e. Integer
7.7	*Number* with one decimal place
£7.66	*Currency* with two decimal places
7.66%	*Percentage* with two decimal places

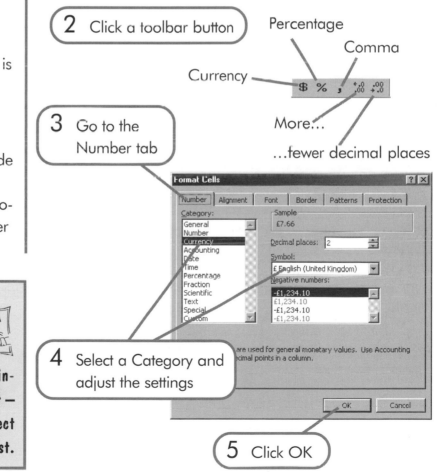

2 Click a toolbar button

Percentage

Comma

Currency

More...

...fewer decimal places

3 Go to the Number tab

4 Select a Category and adjust the settings

5 Click OK

Copying formulae

Many spreadsheets need you to repeat the same calculation across a number of columns or rows, e.g. totals for monthly expenditure, average rainfall over years, final exam results for 30 different children, etc.

Excel takes out the tedium by allowing you to copy formulae to other cells accurately. It uses *relative cell references*, i.e. the relative positions of the cells.

In the example below, the instruction in B6 can be translated as 'sum the contents of the four cells *above* the active cell' which results in the addition of the contents of B2, B3, B4 and B5. If this instruction is then copied to C6, it will result in the addition of the contents of C2, C3, C4 and C5.

❑ Using the mouse

1 Enter the formula or data into the first cell.

2 Move the pointer over the black box in the bottom, right-hand corner of the cell (the fill handle) until it changes to a black cross.

3 Click and drag the cross in the direction for copying. Dotted lines will appear round the cells.

4 Let go and the totals or repeated entries will appear.

5 For copied formulae, click one new total to check that the formula refers to the appropriate column or row.

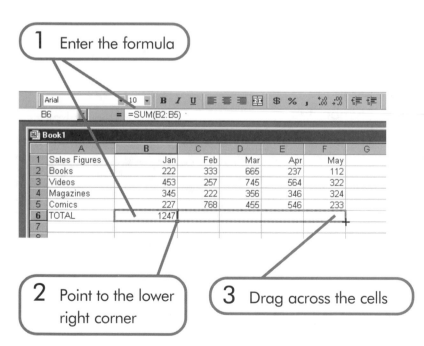

1 Enter the formula

2 Point to the lower right corner

3 Drag across the cells

	A	B	C	D	E	F	G
1	Sales Figures	Jan	Feb	Mar	Apr	May	
2	Books	222	333	665	237	112	
3	Videos	453	257	745	564	322	
4	Magazines	345	222	356	346	324	
5	Comics	227	768	455	546	233	
6	TOTAL	1247					
7							

B6 = =SUM(B2:B5)

Basic steps

Using the menu

1 Enter the first formula or other data and then select this cell and all the cells in the range to take the copied entry.

2 Go to Edit – Fill and select the direction for copying, or Series to copy different types of entry in specific steps.

3 For Series, specify the Type, Step and Stop values as appropriate.

❑ You can also move or copy entries using Cut/ Copy and Paste, just as you do in word-processing, or you can drag selected entries to a new position when the mouse pointer shows an arrow. Hold down [Control] to copy rather than move the contents as you drag.

Fill Series

In most cases, copying text or numbers will fill all the selected cells with the same entry. However, if you enter a date e.g. January or Monday, copying will continue the date series automatically.

If you want to copy numbers by incremental steps, either enter *two* consecutive numbers and select both cells before copying from the second with the pointer, or use the **Edit – Fill – Series** option.

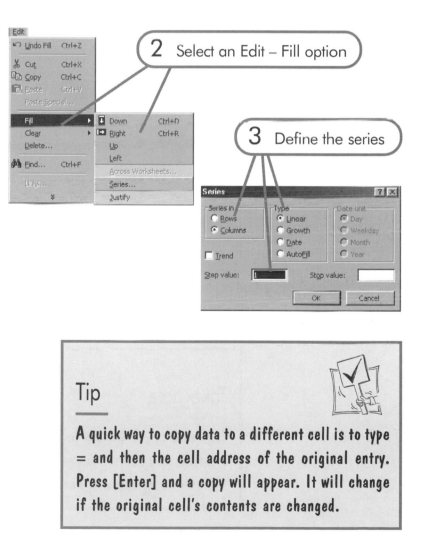

2 Select an Edit – Fill option

3 Define the series

Tip

A quick way to copy data to a different cell is to type = and then the cell address of the original entry. Press [Enter] and a copy will appear. It will change if the original cell's contents are changed.

Absolute cell references

Where you don't want the contents of a particular cell in a formula to change during copying, e.g. if it contains a set percentage, unit of measurement or exchange rate etc., you have to 'fix' its position. In Excel, you do this by marking it with $ signs. You can then copy formulae to reflect changing rows or columns and the address of the cell you have marked remains *Absolute*.

1 Type the formula

	A	B	C	D	E	F
	E6	▼	=	=D6*C1		
	Book1					
1		Discount	10%			
2						
3	Items	Costs(£)	Number	Total	Discount	Final price
4	Fish	5.00	3	15	1.5	13.5
5	Dog	15.00	1	15	1.5	13.5
6	Cat	10.50	2	21	2.1	18.9
7	Bird	5.75	6	34.5	3.45	31.05
8						
9						

2 Type the $ signs or press [F4]

1 Enter the formula in the first cell as normal.

2 Add $ signs automatically to the cell you wish to set as absolute by clicking between its address letter and number in the formula bar and pressing [F4].

Or

3 Type the $ signs in front of the letter and number of the cell you wish to fix as you enter its address into your formula.

4 Press [Enter] to accept the formula and then copy down or across in the usual way.

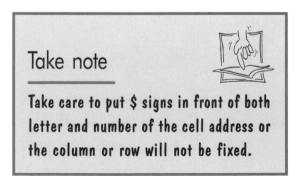

Take note

Take care to put $ signs in front of both letter and number of the cell address or the column or row will not be fixed.

Basic steps

❑ Inserting columns or rows

1 Click the column header to the *right* of the position for a new column. The complete column will be selected.

2 Select Insert – Column and a new column will slide into place.

3 Select more than one column to insert that number of new ones.

4 For a new row, select as many rows as you want to insert, *below* the new row position.

❑ Deleting columns and rows

5 Select the column/row.

6 Open the Edit menu and select Delete.

Adjusting the grid

If you want to insert new columns or rows into a spreadsheet, the letter or number headings are adjusted automatically and the new columns or rows appear to 'slide' into place. This adjustment also occurs if you delete columns or rows.

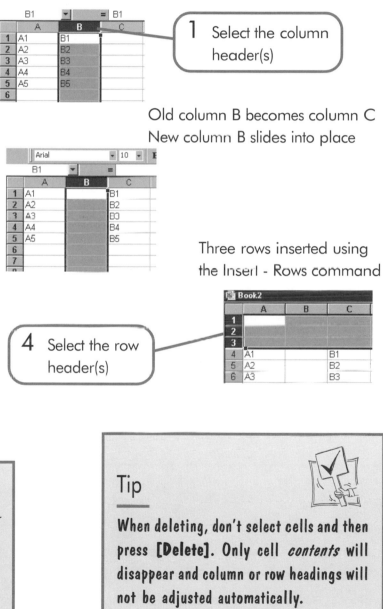

1 Select the column header(s)

Old column B becomes column C
New column B slides into place

Three rows inserted using the Insert - Rows command

4 Select the row header(s)

Take note

If you select only one cell, you can choose to shift cells or delete the entire column or row.

Tip

When deleting, don't select cells and then press [Delete]. Only cell *contents* will disappear and column or row headings will not be adjusted automatically.

83

Column and row sizes

Quite often you will find that the standard width of columns or height of rows is not right for displaying your data. It is very easy to change the measurements – either by dragging with the mouse or using the menus.

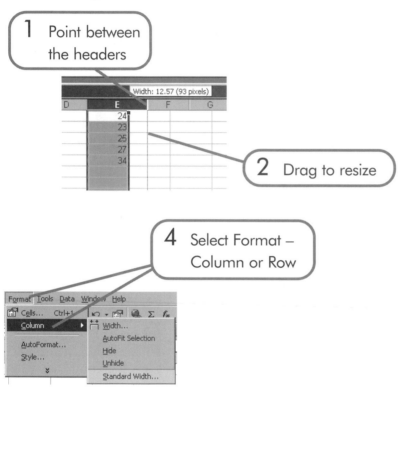

1 Point between the headers

Width: 12.57 (93 pixels)

2 Drag to resize

4 Select Format – Column or Row

Format Tools Data Window Help

Cells... Ctrl+1
Column ▶
  Width...
  AutoFit Selection
AutoFormat... Hide
Style... Unhide
  Standard Width...

Tip

If you see ### appear, it means the column is not wide enough to display the full entry. Just widen the column and the symbols will disappear.

1 To widen a column, move the pointer between its header and the one to its right.

2 When it shows a 2-way arrow, click and drag the edge of the box to the right. If it is too wide, drag to the left.

3 For rows, drag the lower edge of the row-header up or down with the 2-way arrow.

Or

4 Select the column or row, and use Format – Column/Row to open the dialog box.

5 Enter an exact measure into the Width/Height box.

Or

6 Select AutoFit so the column /row fits the widest/highest entry.

Or

7 Select Standard Width to return to the default measurement.

Borders and shading

1 Select the cells to be
   formatted.

2 Click the Border drop-
   down arrow and select
   an option to add boxes
   or single edge borders.

3 Go to Format – Cells –
   Border to choose new
   line styles and colours,
   and apply them to one
   or more borders.

4 Select a background
   colour from the Fill
   Colour palette on the
   toolbar, or add a
   pattern from the For-
   mat – Cells – Patterns
   menu.

You can add borders or shading to individual cells, or apply these to all the data on a spreadsheet. Excel has a range of styles ready to select or customize via the **Format – AutoFormat** menu. You can also use the Borders and Fill Colour toolbar shortcuts or select a wider range of options from the **Format – Cells – Border** or **Patterns** menu tabs.

No borders

4 Set the Fill colour

2 Add a simple border

3 Open the Format Cells Border
   dialog box to define the border

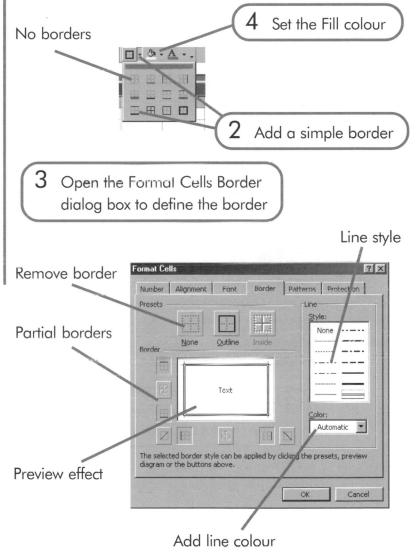

Line style

Remove border

Partial borders

Preview effect

Add line colour

Tip

If you see a line in one cell that you cannot remove, it may be a border added by mistake. Just select the cell and click the Border option showing no lines.

Applying an AutoFormat

It may be easier to apply a ready-made design to your spreadsheet that includes borders, shading and font styles. There is a range of styles available in Excel and you can even customise the designs by limiting which formats to apply.

Basic steps

1 Select the spreadsheet cells and go to Format – AutoFormat.

2 Scroll down the examples until you find one you want to apply.

3 Click off any boxes in the Format to apply section to prevent that option being applied.

4 Click OK.

5 Back in your spreadsheet, use the Format menu to amend colours or fonts.

1 Open the AutoFormat dialog box

2 Select a format

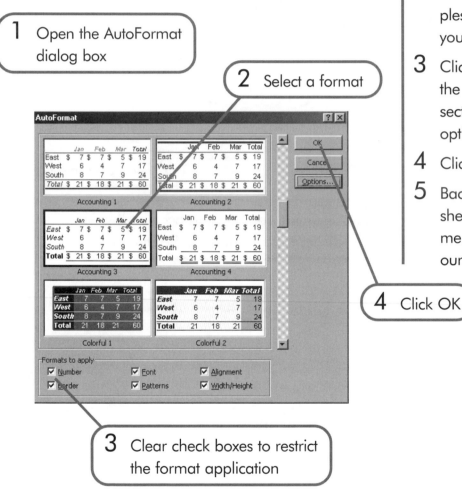

4 Click OK

3 Clear check boxes to restrict the format application

Headers and footers

1 Select Page Set up –
Header/Footer.

2 Select a Header from
the drop-down list.

Or

3 Click Custom Header.

4 Click in the left, centre
or right section to
position the header
then enter text, or insert
the date or page
number.

5 To format text, select it
and click the Font tool.

6 Click OK to return to
the Page Setup to close
or preview the header,
or to create a footer in
the same way.

To add the date, your name or page numbers to your printouts,
you can insert headers and footers. These are available from the
File – Page Set up dialog box and you can either enter text
directly, or insert options using the toolbar buttons.

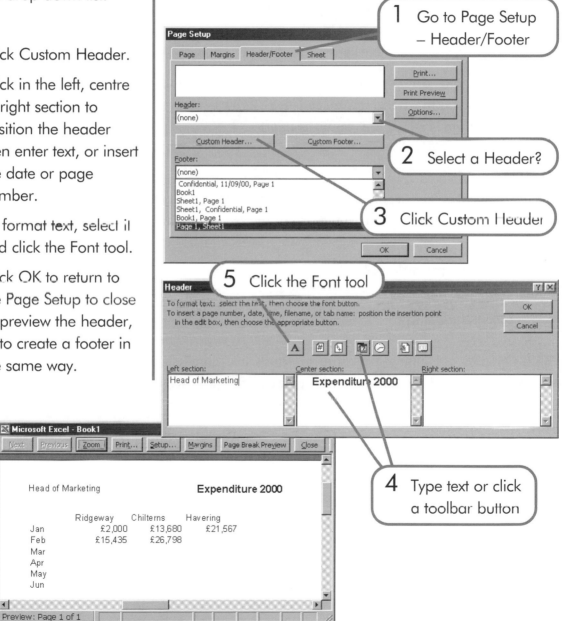

Creating a database

Databases are collections of items such as books, names and addresses, evening classes or houses for sale that are organised in a systematic way and can be sorted or searched. Unlike Microsoft Access, Excel is not a relational database application and doesn't have many of the complex facilities offered by purpose-built database software. However, it can be perfectly adequate for creating simple databases for everyday use.

In a database, each row containing data relating to one item in your collection is known as a *record*, and the first row headings under which data is stored are known as *fields*.

Sort records

The contents of cells in a column can be re-ordered very easily by selecting the column and clicking one of the A - Z toolbar buttons.

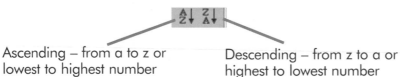

Ascending – from a to z or lowest to highest number

Descending – from z to a or highest to lowest number

With columns containing a mixture of words and numbers, numbers are sorted first, and you need to take care that no spaces have been left in front of any entry as this affects the order of sort.

Although records in a database can be entered in any order on the spreadsheet, you may want to sort them so that they are listed in order of one field such as price, location or number of bedrooms. If you select the complete range of cells and click an A–Z toolbar button, the sort will be based on the data in the first field on the left. If this is not the appropriate field, or you want different levels of sort, you need to use the **Data – Sort** menu.

Tip

If you want to create more sophisticated databases, learn how to use Microsoft Access by reading *Access Made Simple.*

Tip

Never select a single column in a database to sort or you will split up data relating to individual records and make nonsense of the information.

Basic steps

❑ Sorting a database

1 Select the range of cells to be sorted and click the appropriate A–Z toolbar button.

Or

2 To select a particular first-level column, or combine up to three levels of sort, select the cells and then go to Data – Sort.

3 Select the first column on which to base the sort from the list in the Sort by box, e.g. town, in ascending order.

4 If necessary, add one or two further levels of sort, e.g. first by town, then by price and then by bedrooms.

5 If you selected field headings, click the *Header row* option under My list has, to remove the field names from the sort.

6 Click OK.

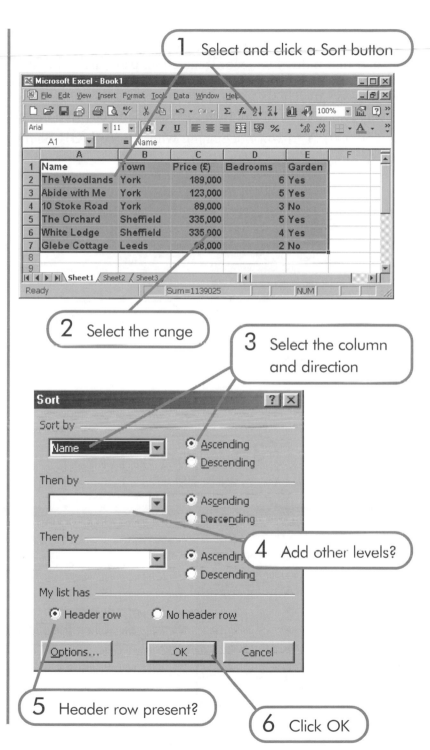

1 Select and click a Sort button

2 Select the range

3 Select the column and direction

4 Add other levels?

5 Header row present?

6 Click OK

89

Finding records

If you use the Form function, you can display one record at a time and find individual records matching particular criteria.

Entries can be matched exactly, or you can customise the search by using expressions in any field such as >50,000 (*Price* more than £50,000), Y* (*Town* beginning with Y), York **OR** Sheffield (in either of these two towns) etc.

- ❑ Using a form to find records
1. Select all the cells in the database.
2. Go to Data – Form and click the Criteria button.
3. In any of the empty field boxes, enter exact words or numbers, or your own expression, to find records matching the entry.
4. Click Find Previous or Find Next to work through the database locating matching records one at a time. For each record displayed, you will see which numbered record has been found.

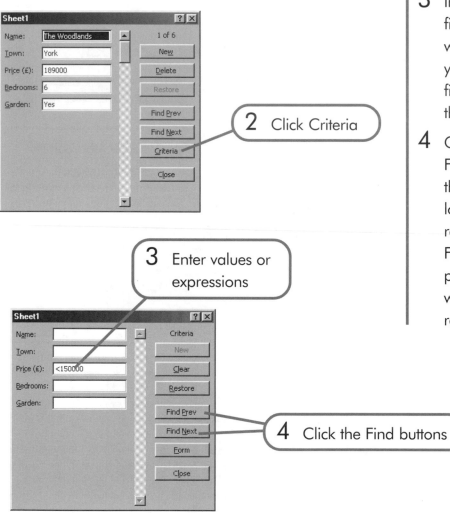

2 Click Criteria

3 Enter values or expressions

4 Click the Find buttons

Filtering records

1 Select the cells and go to Data – Filter – AutoFilter.

2 Each field name cell now has an arrow that you can click to drop down a list of all the entries in that field.

3 For any field, select the match from the list or click Custom.

4 In the Custom dialog box, select a logical operator, e.g. *is greater than*, *begins with*, etc. then enter your own data or select from the drop-down list in the right-hand pane.

5 Click OK and you will see a subset of the records in the database meeting this criterion.

6 Repeat with different criteria until you see just those records meeting all your criteria.

7 To return to the full database, select Data – AutoFilter – Show All.

To display several records e.g. all houses with a garden, or all homes in York under £100,000, you can carry out a search using the AutoFilter command.

When filtering, the subset of records that is displayed can be printed or copied to a new location, or you can remove the filter and show all the records again.

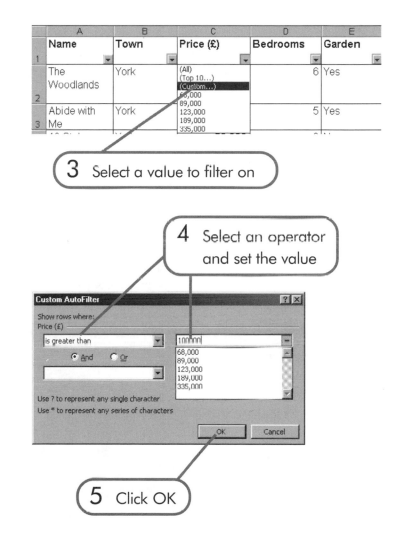

3 Select a value to filter on

4 Select an operator and set the value

5 Click OK

Printing

You can print spreadsheets with or without gridlines, change to landscape orientation if some columns go over the page, or make sure you only print on one page by selecting *Fit to 1 page* to reduce the font size. All these options are available from the **File – Page Set up – Page** or **Sheet** menu.

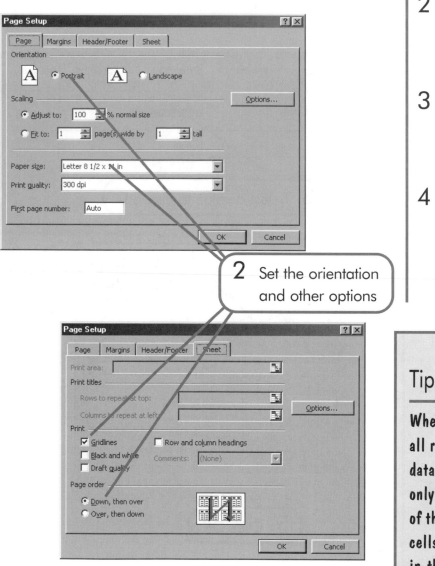

2 Set the orientation and other options

Basic steps

1 Check print preview, and if relevant go to Page Break Preview to alter the position for a page break.

2 Change orientation or make other changes using the File – Page Set up options.

3 For one copy of the data on the current sheet, click the Print toolbar button.

4 Go to File – Print to change to another printer, print several copies or print selected sheets.

Tip

When printing, you will print all rows and columns in which data has been entered. If you only want to print a small part of the spreadsheet, select the cells and then click *Selection* in the Print What box.

Creating charts

1 Select the data and its headings for the chart.

2 Click the Chart Wizard toolbar button.

3 Step 1: Select a chart type and preview its appearance before clicking Next.

4 Step 2: Select the data series – depending on whether you want row or column headings to form the X-axis labels, and if necessary, amend the Data range.

To display numerical information graphically, you can create a chart with the help of Excel's Chart Wizard. Choose from 2-D or 3-D column, bar, line, pie or less well-known chart types. You can add your own titles and either place the chart on its own sheet or 'float' it over your spreadsheet data.

The Chart Wizard makes columns or rows of values into separate data series that are named in the legend.

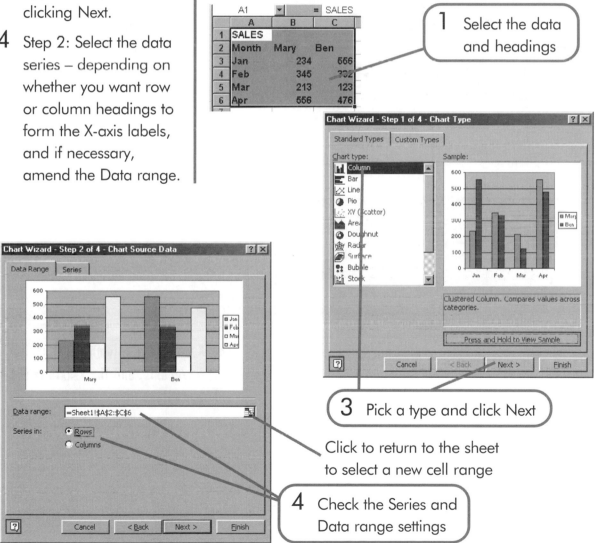

1 Select the data and headings

3 Pick a type and click Next

Click to return to the sheet to select a new cell range

4 Check the Series and Data range settings

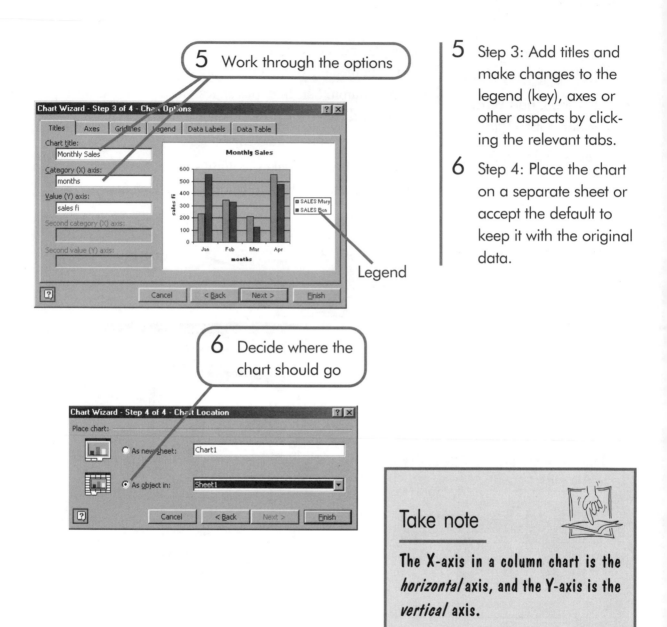

5 Work through the options

6 Decide where the chart should go

Legend

5 Step 3: Add titles and make changes to the legend (key), axes or other aspects by clicking the relevant tabs.

6 Step 4: Place the chart on a separate sheet or accept the default to keep it with the original data.

Take note

The X-axis in a column chart is the *horizontal* axis, and the Y-axis is the *vertical* axis.

Basic steps

Amending and printing charts

1 Use the Chart toolbar options, e.g. to delete the legend, change chart type or angle selected text.

2 To open the Format dialog box and amend colours, fonts, number styles, alignment, etc. of an element, right-click on it and select Format from the short menu; or use the Chart toolbar to select the element then click the Format button.

3 Right-click the data or chart area to add trend lines or amend the source data.

4 Select the chart to print it alone.

5 De-select to print it together with the spreadsheet data.

The chart appears 'selected' i.e. showing black squares (sizing handles) on the borders, and in this state it can be re-sized, moved or deleted in the same way as drawings or pictures. You can also format a selected chart using menu options or the chart toolbar that will have appeared. Clicking outside the chart de-selects it, and clicking inside will select it again.

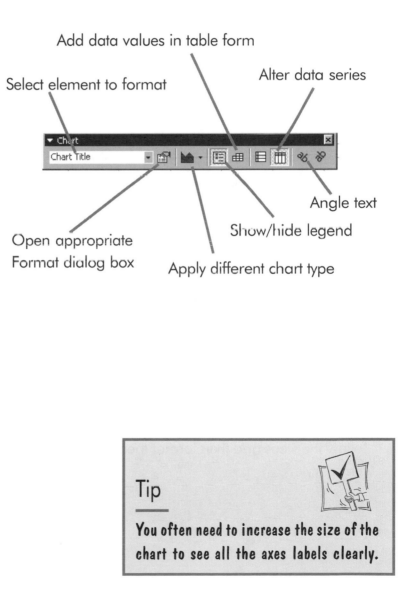

Add data values in table form

Select element to format

Alter data series

Open appropriate Format dialog box

Show/hide legend

Apply different chart type

Angle text

Tip

You often need to increase the size of the chart to see all the axes labels clearly.

Summary

❑ Spreadsheets are made up of hundreds of cells ar-
    ranged in columns and rows. Cell addresses combine
    column heading letters and row heading numbers.

❑ You can use Excel to perform calculations, and the
    resultant data can be displayed in grids or used to
    create charts.

❑ Formulae always start with the equals sign and must
    be entered using correct operators. If they include cell
    addresses, rather than raw data, amending the data in
    the cell will result in an automatic update of your
    results.

❑ Text or numbers can be formatted to improve the
    appearance of the spreadsheet, and columns and
    rows can be inserted or deleted if you need to change
    your display. You can also add borders or shading or
    apply one of the design templates available.

❑ To save time, formulae can be copied across columns
    or rows as they make use of relative cell referencing.
    However, you need to 'absolute' cell addresses where
    these must remain constant.

❑ Spreadsheets can be printed with or without gridlines,
    small enough to fit one page and alone or with an
    accompanying chart.

❑ Charts are easy to produce using a Wizard. You just
    follow the steps and then format them in your pre-
    ferred style.

6 Presentations

PowerPoint presentations

Everyone feels more comfortable giving talks when supported by good quality audiovisual aids. Using a presentation package such as Microsoft PowerPoint allows you to produce beautifully illustrated slides for printing on acetate sheets or running on the computer. They can include animation or sound effects and can be supported by various handouts and notes.

When you start PowerPoint, you are presented with four choices.

> **AutoContent Wizard**: Gives you a presentation that will contain 7 or 8 slides. Their contents will have to be replaced with your own choice of text and graphics.

> **Design Template**: This offers a choice of background designs alone, or selecting a complete presentation to customise.

> **Blank presentation** (the default): This is the best choice if you want to start small and design a slide at a time.

> **Open an existing presentation**: Once you have created and saved presentations, you must click this option to select a named file from the list or browse through presentations on your computer.

1 Click the PowerPoint icon , or select the application from the Start – Programs menu.

2 Select an option from the PowerPoint dialog box.

3 Click OK.

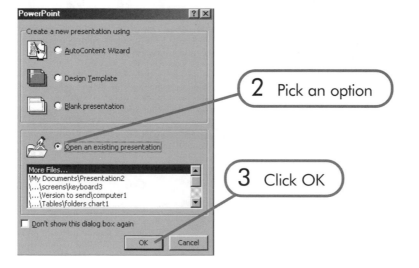

2 Pick an option

3 Click OK

Basic steps

Creating a presentation

1 Scroll through the different layouts in the New Slide box to find a suitable first slide for your presentation.

2 Choose a blank slide, or select one including one or more 'place-holders' (specific areas already in place for pictures, columns, charts or headings).

3 Click OK .

4 You will now see your slide in the top, right pane of the screen.

5 Whichever layout you select, you can change this at any time by clicking the Slide Layout button 🔲 or going to Format – Slide Layout and applying an alter-native layout.

PowerPoint opens in Normal view. If you select the Blank Database option, you will see three different panes and a New Slide box superimposed on top. Once a particular slide layout is selected and you click OK, or if you open an existing presentation, you can start work on your presentation in any of the three panes.

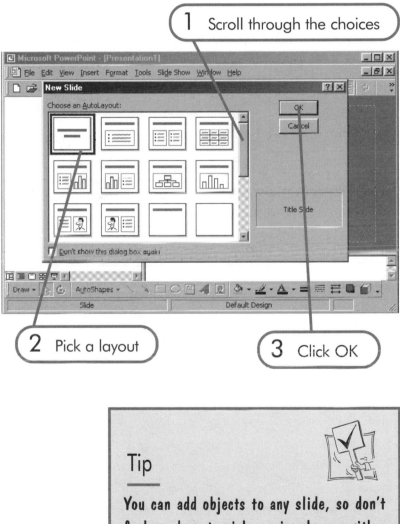

1 Scroll through the choices

2 Pick a layout

3 Click OK

Tip

You can add objects to any slide, so don't feel you have to pick one in advance with a placeholder for charts or pictures.

Building up your slides

Once your first slide is in place, you can add others at any time. As you build up your slides, you will need to go between them and possibly change their order. You will also want to view them in different ways, to see how the whole presentation is looking.

❑ To add a new slide

1 Click the New Slide toolbar button ⬚ , or select this option from the Common Tasks button or Insert menu.

2 Select the layout and click OK. A new slide will appear on screen and you can start entering text or images.

3 Continue adding slides until you have the correct number for your presentation.

4 To go between your slides, click the navigation arrows to the right of the slide.

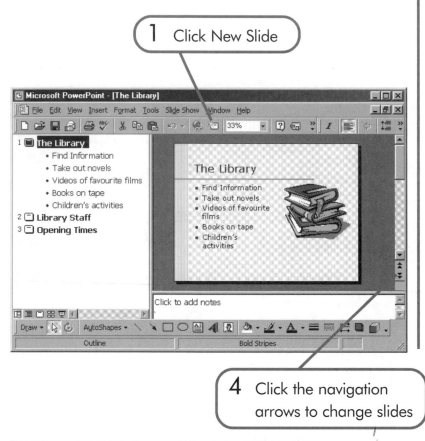

1 Click New Slide

4 Click the navigation arrows to change slides

Tip

To learn how to animate presentations, run slide shows and use other advanced features of PowerPoint, read *PowerPoint Made Simple.*

Different views

1 Click one of the toolbar View buttons, or select from the View menu.

2 Whichever slide is selected in Outline or Slide Sorter view will be displayed when you change to Normal, Slide or Notes view.

3 If you are watching a Slide Show, run through slides by pressing Page Up or Down or clicking the mouse, and exit by pressing [Esc].

There are five **View** toolbar buttons:

▣ **Normal** to work on one of three panes that are all visible on screen together;

▤ **Outline** to work with just the text of any slide;

▢ **Slide** to change the look as well as the text of a slide;

▦ **Slide Sorter** to see the complete presentation on screen;

▣ **Slide Show** to allow you to step through your presentation to see how it would look when run on a computer.

You can also select **View – Notes Page** to type in speaker's notes below a slide image, or **View – Master – Slide Master** to add text or objects that will then appear on all your slides.

Normal view

Outline pane ────

Outline view

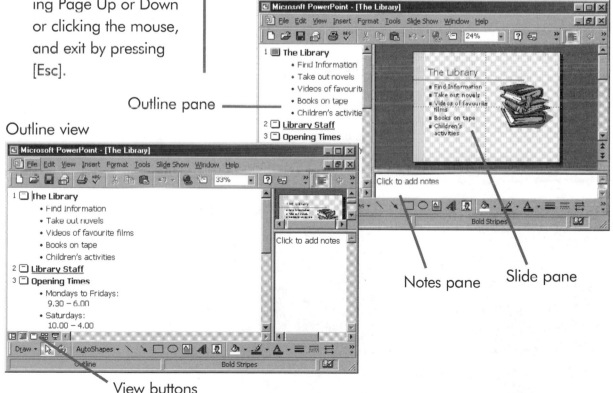

Notes pane   Slide pane

View buttons

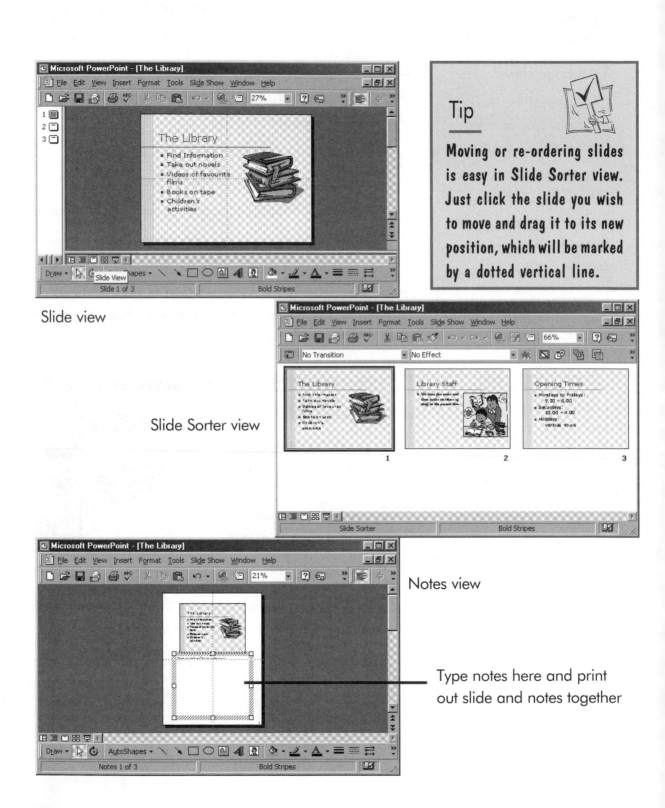

Slide view

Tip

Moving or re-ordering slides is easy in Slide Sorter view. Just click the slide you wish to move and drag it to its new position, which will be marked by a dotted vertical line.

Slide Sorter view

Notes view

Type notes here and print out slide and notes together

Basic steps

1 Click in the placeholder and enter text as usual. Press [Enter] to add a new line within the same box.

2 For blank slides or areas, click the Text Box button on the Drawing toolbar and then click in place on the slide.

3 Start typing in the box – it will expand to provide room for the text.

Adding text

You have two options with text: using placeholders and clicking directly in the boxes provided, or adding a text box to any part of the slide.

To change the default formatting, select the text and then use the **Format** menu options or toolbar buttons just as you would in word processing.

There are some extra options that can be particularly useful:

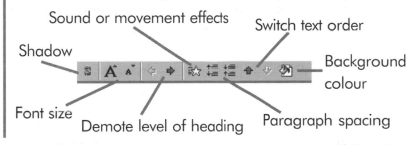

Sound or movement effects

Switch text order

Shadow

Background colour

Font size

Demote level of heading

Paragraph spacing

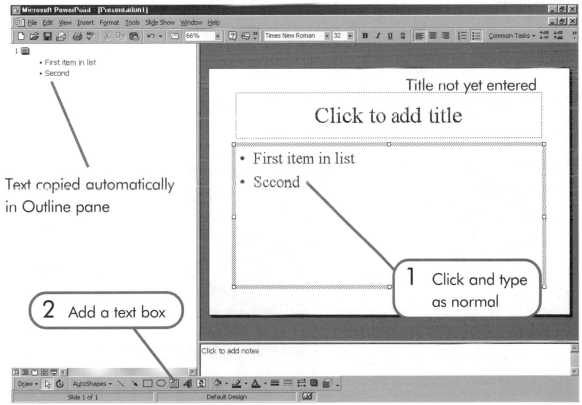

Text copied automatically in Outline pane

2 Add a text box

1 Click and type as normal

Altering text boxes

Text boxes used in PowerPoint do not usually have borders showing when you have completed text entry. If these appear and aren't wanted, remove them by selecting the box border, click the Line Color button and select No Line.

Otherwise, enhance the slide by choosing from a wide range of colours, widths and style of line to surround your text. You can also change the size of the text box and move it to different parts of the slide by clicking to show the sizing handles and dragging with a 2-way arrow (to re-size) or 4-way arrow (to move).

Basic steps

1 To select a text box, click on the text to pick up an invisible box, then click on one of the box edges.

2 A selected text box has a thick, textured edge with small boxes (sizing handles) around it.

3 Use the Drawing toolbar options to change its lines and backgrounds (fill).

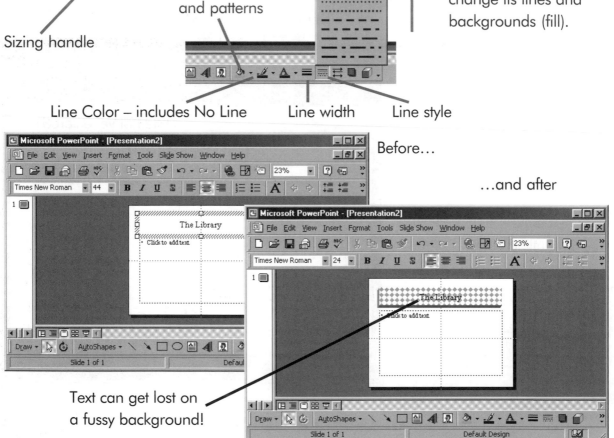

Introduction

Sizing handle

Fill effects – include colours, textures and patterns

Line Color – includes No Line   Line width   Line style

Before…

…and after

Text can get lost on a fussy background!

104

Basic steps

1 Click the Word Art button ◀ on the Drawing toolbar.

2 Select a style from the WordArt Gallery.

3 Click OK.

4 In the editing box, type in your text.

5 Select the font and size, and set Bold or Italic if wanted.

6 Click OK.

cont...

Although you can change font types, styles, colours and sizes in normal text boxes, you can have more fun with words if you create them in Word Art.

These words can be shaped, stretched, shaded and blocked and given unusual colour effects. They are very useful for pasting across your slide at angles, or for special-effect titles.

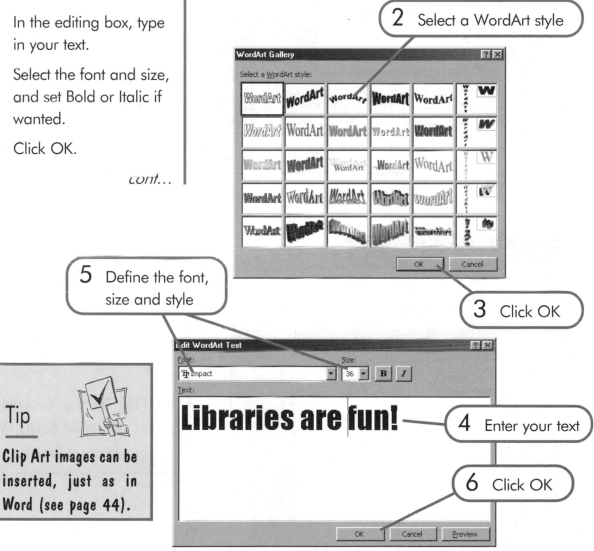

2 Select a WordArt style

3 Click OK

5 Define the font, size and style

4 Enter your text

6 Click OK

Libraries are fun!

Tip

Clip Art images can be inserted, just as in Word (see page 44).

The WordArt appears on the slide

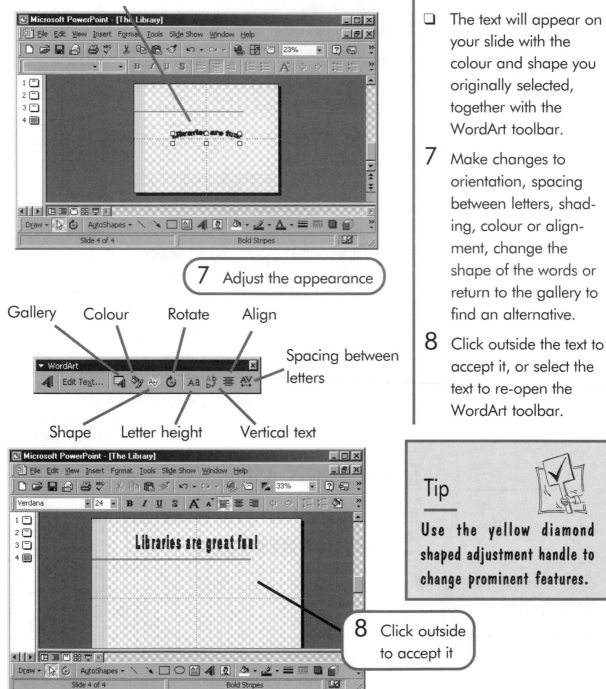

7 Adjust the appearance

Gallery   Colour   Rotate   Align

Spacing between letters

Shape   Letter height   Vertical text

cont...

❑ The text will appear on your slide with the colour and shape you originally selected, together with the WordArt toolbar.

7 Make changes to orientation, spacing between letters, shading, colour or alignment, change the shape of the words or return to the gallery to find an alternative.

8 Click outside the text to accept it, or select the text to re-open the WordArt toolbar.

Tip

Use the yellow diamond shaped adjustment handle to change prominent features.

8 Click outside to accept it

Charts and other objects

1   Double-click the Chart placeholder or select Insert – Picture and click Organization Chart.

2   If you prefer a different layout, select an alternative from the Styles menu.

3   Click in a box and enter your own choice of text.

4   To remove an unwanted box, select it and press [Delete].

5   Return to your slide by selecting File – Close and return to (*Presentation name*), making sure you save the chart by clicking Yes to update the object in the presentation.

PowerPoint has access to a range of applications that can be used to add visual effects to your slides. Some of these are available directly from the **Insert** menu, but they and many more can be accessed if you select **Insert – Object** and scroll through the applications listed.

Organization Charts

This application allows you to present hierarchical information such as family trees or company management structures very easily. You create the chart using Microsoft Organization Chart and the finished chart is then saved and embedded in your slide. If you need to edit the chart, double click it to link up with the application again and use the toolbar and menu options to make your changes.

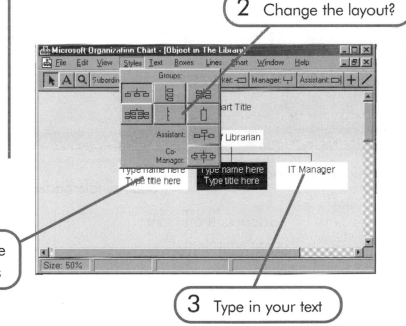

2   Change the layout?

4   Select and delete unwanted boxes

3   Type in your text

Customising an Organisation Chart

A range of box types is available if you want to build up your hierarchy and add a new member e.g. an assistant or subordinate. You will also find a full range of formatting tools to let you apply different colours, backgrounds and fonts to your chart to enhance its appearance.

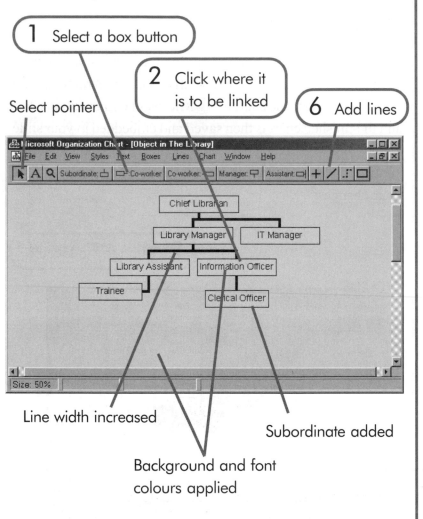

1 Select a box button

2 Click where it is to be linked

6 Add lines

Select pointer

Line width increased

Subordinate added

Background and font colours applied

Basic steps

❑ To add a new box

1 Click the toolbar button showing the new relationship. The pointer will now display the symbol on the button.

2 Click the box to which the new box will be linked.

❑ Formatting

3 To change box borders or colour options use the Boxes menu. (Select more than one box by first drawing an outline round them with the Select pointer.)

4 Use the Text menu to alter fonts and the Lines menu to alter connecting lines.

5 Choose a background colour from the Chart menu.

6 Add extra lines, e.g. to link boxes by clicking a toolbar button and dragging across the chart.

Basic steps

1 Double click a place-holder showing a chart, click the toolbar button or select Insert – Chart to take you to the chart application.

2 Click on the spread-sheet to amend text or numerical data, and add your own title.

3 To change the chart type, select from Chart – Chart Type and preview the effect of the change before clicking OK.

4 To insert or format fonts, alignment, leg-end (key), colours of lines etc., right-click on the relevant data, axis or title and select from the shortcut menu.

5 To return to your slide, click once *outside* the chart. To return for amendments, double-click the chart itself.

Numerical charts

To display numerical data visually, you can use one of the charting applications available from PowerPoint, e.g. Microsoft Graph 2000 Chart. Replace the sample data and edit or format the chart to insert it into your presentation.

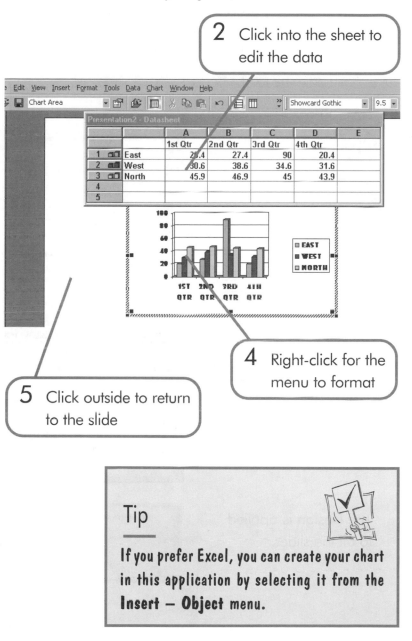

2 Click into the sheet to edit the data

4 Right-click for the menu to format

5 Click outside to return to the slide

Tip

If you prefer Excel, you can create your chart in this application by selecting it from the **Insert – Object** menu.

Slide design

Rather than have a white background for your slides, you can add colours, patterns and special features or use one of the design templates available. You can also decide whether to have a different design for each slide, or standardize your presentation and give every slide the same 'look'.

❑ Applying a Design Template

1 Select any slide and then go to Format – Apply Design Template.

2 Preview the range of designs.

3 Select one and click Apply.

❑ All your slides will now have that same colour and layout.

1 Go to Apply Design Template

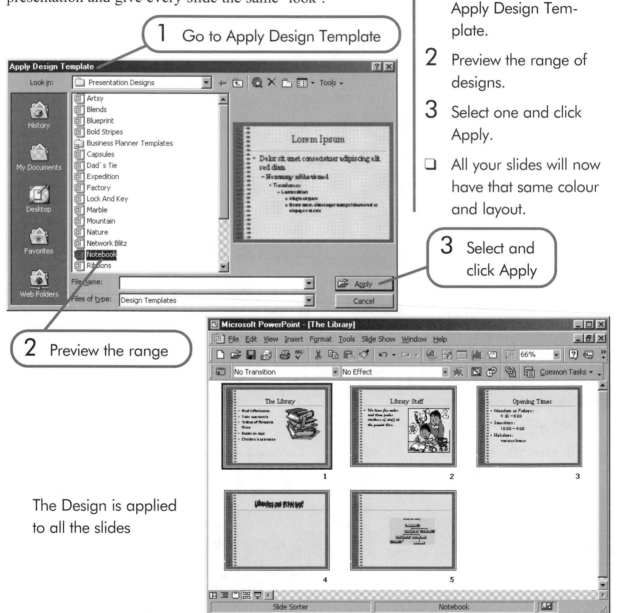

3 Select and click Apply

2 Preview the range

The Design is applied to all the slides

Basic steps

1 Select a slide and go to Format – Background.

2 Click the arrow to display alternative colours, but choose More Colors for a wider choice.

3 Open the Fill Effects dialog box if you want to select patterns or textures for your background.

4 Click Apply to All to change the background for all your slides.

Or

5 Apply to change only the original slide you selected.

6 Select Format – Slide Colour Scheme to alter the relative colour mix for text and background.

Customising slide designs

If you want a different colour scheme for an individual slide, or you want to amend some of the design template features, you can apply different colours or patterns using the **Format** menu.

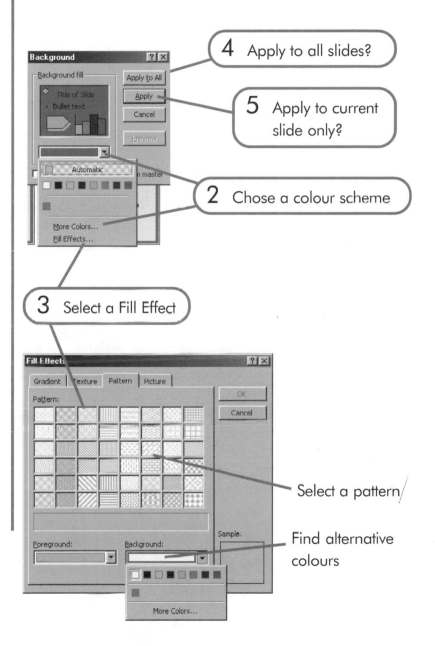

4 Apply to all slides?

5 Apply to current slide only?

2 Chose a colour scheme

3 Select a Fill Effect

Select a pattern

Find alternative colours

Slide Master

The *Slide Master* controls the basic features of your slides such as the text formatting or background. It also contains placeholders for titles and main text, dates, footers and slide numbers This means that, if you want to change bullet styles or include a logo or the date on every slide, you don't need to amend each slide in turn. Make the changes to the master slide and your whole presentation will be updated automatically.

Basic steps

1 Go to View – Master – Slide Master.

2 Select and format the title or lower levels of text in the normal way.

3 Click on the text and select Format – Bullets and Numbering to change bullet styles for the presentation.

4 To add dates or slide numbers to all slides, use the marked areas.

Or

5 Click View – Header and Footer and complete the boxes.

6 To place an object on all slides, insert it on the Slide Master.

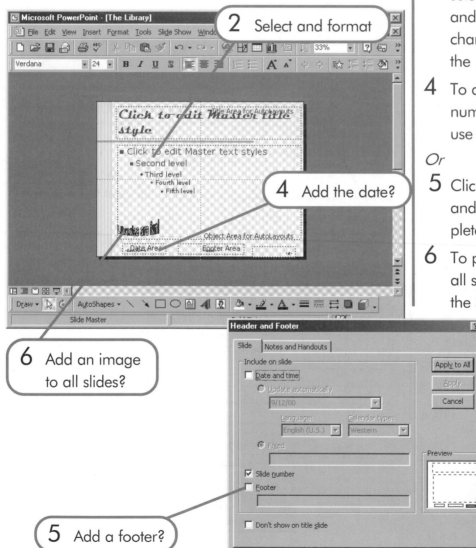

Basic steps

1 Save presentations in the normal way by completing the Save As dialog box with the name of the file and location.

2 Go to File – Page Set up to select the orientation and size.

3 Select File – Print for any printing options other than one copy of all the slides.

4 Choose whether to print slides, handouts, notes or an outline.

5 Select the arrangement of images on your handouts.

Tip

If printing for overhead projectors, make sure the acetate sheets are suitable for your printer.

Saving and printing

Once you have done any work on a presentation, you need to save it onto a floppy disk or into a suitable folder on your hard disk. You should save regularly so that you maintain an updated version of the presentation.

A single presentation file contains all the slides, outlines, notes etc. that you have prepared together, and you save in exactly the same way as you save Word documents.

Printing is different as you can choose what you print, and you will need to sct the appropriate orientation and size from the Page Set up dialog box.

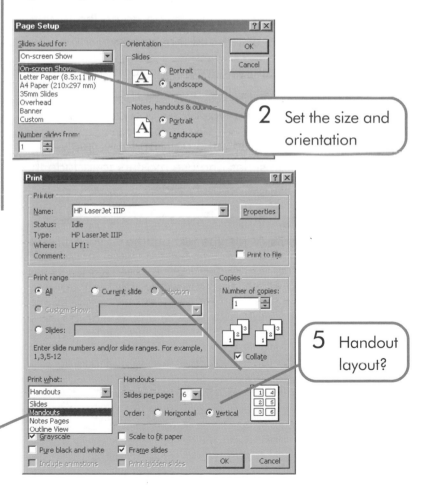

2 Set the size and orientation

5 Handout layout?

4 Choose what to print

Summary

- ❑ With PowerPoint you can produce slides and supporting material to enhance your presentations.

- ❑ You can run a slide show on the computer or print onto overhead projector transparencies or paper.

- ❑ There are presentation templates you can adapt, or you can create your own slide by slide. Each slide you add can be selected from a range of layouts, but you can change these as you work and start with a blank slide if you prefer.

- ❑ Placeholders make it easy to add text, charts or pictures to your slides, but objects can be added to any slide and moved or re-sized if necessary.

- ❑ As well as the usual text formatting tools, there are extra facilities to enable you to add special effects, and WordArt is a different type of text you can include.

- ❑ To give your presentation a uniform look, apply one design to all the slides and use masters to include the same text or image on every slide.

- ❑ When printing, you can choose to produce slides, notes, handouts or just the text outline of your presentation.

7 The Internet

Getting connected

If your computer has a modem – a piece of hardware that enables you to connect to the Internet via a normal telephone line – you will be able to find information and communicate via the international network of computers known as the Internet.

The World Wide Web

Often referred to as the Web, this is the name given to the linked multimedia documents that have been loaded onto the Internet and that offer anything from film clips, medical articles, stock market information and weather reports to goods and services you can buy without leaving your own home.

Connecting

To connect to the Internet and search the Web, you need an Internet Access or Service Provider (ISP) and the software to view Web pages known as a *browser*. Today, some ISPs charge a monthly fee that includes a set number of free hours online, but the majority offer a free connection and you pay for all the phone calls. You should find ISP CD-ROMs in shops or magazines. Follow the instructions on the CD-ROM and you will install all the software you need, including one of the two well-known browsers – Netscape or Internet Explorer.

1 Double-click the ISP or browser icon on your Desktop.

2 You may see a Web page from your ISP.

3 A small computer icon will be seen flashing on the Taskbar to show you are connected to the Internet.

Tip

Where access to the Internet is free, watch the clock when seeking technical support by telephone, as you can be charged over 50p per minute.

1 Double-click the browser icon to connect

Internet Explorer

Basic steps

Saving money

1 To finish working on the Internet altogether, close the browser window to open the Disconnect dialog box and click Yes.

2 To keep the present page on screen but go 'offline', double-click the computer icon on the Taskbar and click the Disconnect button. (You may need to open the Connected dialog box via a Dial Up Networking icon.)

As you are likely to pay for every minute you are linked to the Internet, you should work offline as much as possible to keep costs down. If you have accessed a long document you want to read at your leisure, or when you have finished working on the Internet, disconnect to close the telephone connection. You can always reconnect again if you want to access a new site or send or receive messages.

Message you may get when you close the Browser window

Name of ISP

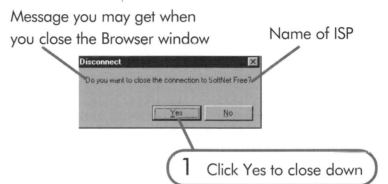

1 Click Yes to close down

Message box when you double-click the computer icon or open Dial up networking

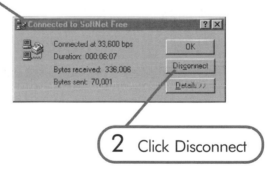

2 Click Disconnect

Web pages

Both browsers have similar menus and toolbar buttons, and these will be visible all the time. In the main window you will see the opening web page known as the 'home page'. Each service provider has its own home page appearing by default, and you will return to this page whenever you click the Home toolbar button.

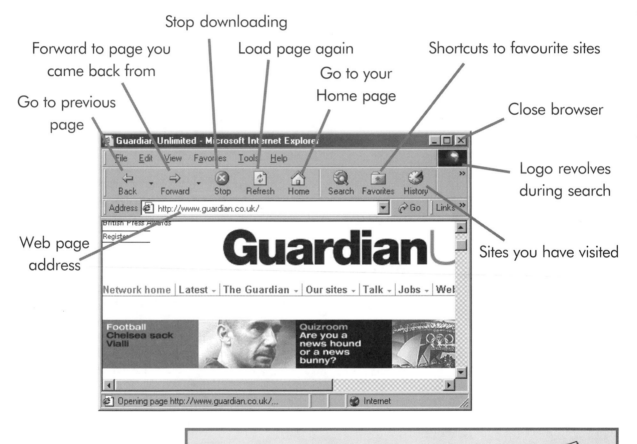

Forward to page you came back from

Stop downloading

Load page again

Go to your Home page

Shortcuts to favourite sites

Go to previous page

Close browser

Logo revolves during search

Web page address

Sites you have visited

Tip

If you find a page you would prefer as your opening screen, you can make it the Home Page. Select **Tools — Internet Options** and on the **General** tab click *Use Current Page* in the **Home Page** area.

Using hyperlinks

Take note

The **Home Page toolbar** button takes you to the page you always open when you connect to the Internet. On a Web page, clicking a Home hyperlink will normally take you to the main index or opening page for that site.

As you move the mouse pointer over a Web page, it will keep changing from the normal arrow to a hand 🖐. Whenever this happens, it means the text or image on which it is resting is a hyperlink. It can be 'clicked' and will then link to another page on the Web. Hyperlink text is often blue and underlined, and changes colour after clicking.

If a hyperlink takes you to a page of no interest, return to the original page by clicking the *Back* toolbar button. Change your mind and *want* to go to that page after all – click the Forward toolbar button to make the link again.

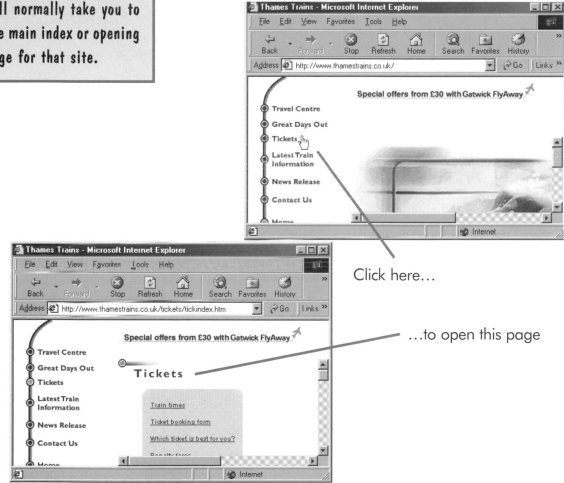

Click here...

...to open this page

Addresses and URLs

The address of any Web page is known as its Uniform Resource Locator (URL). Each URL has several sections and the punctuation between these MUST be entered accurately, although text can be either upper or lower case. For example, the BBC Home Page can be reached by entering

> http://www.bbc.co.uk

http:// is short for hypertext transfer protocol, and means the file is a hypertext document (Web page). You may see other codes on the Web, e.g. **ftp://** for file transfer protocol, that indicates a site from which files can be downloaded.

www. denotes the World Wide Web

bbc is the company name

co.uk shows the type of organisation, i.e. a company in the UK.

The company name and type of organisation elements together form the *domain name*.

Guess the Address

URLS are standardised and you are given certain information by the extension. Common extensions include:

.com   international companies (although increasingly used by British organisations)

.ac.uk   British academic institutions

.edu   American universities and colleges

.gov.uk   governmental sites

.org.uk   organizations such as charities.

This system means that you can often guess the address for an organization – as long as you know its name, location and the type of business.

1 Type the URL into the Address box and press [Enter].

2 Check that the browser logo is revolving to show the connection is being made.

3 If it seems to be taking too long for the page to download, click the Stop button and try again later.

Tip

You don't usually need to type http:// – just start with www.

The best ways to search

1 Connect to the URL for the directory, e.g. www.excite.co.uk

2 Click first choice of category heading.

3 As lists appear, scroll down and click on the most appropriate heading.

A major role for the Web is to provide information. As you can't know the exact location of every Web page holding relevant information, you will need the help of a directory or search engine at some stage. Many organisations offer both types of search on the same site, and popular URLs include www.altavista.co.uk, www.google.com, www.yahoo.co.uk, www.excite.com, www.ukdirectory.co.uk and www.hotbot.com.

Directories

Directories work like a book contents page or library classification system. The companies examine and classify Web pages under various headings and subheadings. You just need to click on a category and work down through the lists that keep appearing until you reach actual Web sites to browse through. Often you have the chance to enter a specific word or phrase to carry out a search within a particular sub-category.

Take note

Although thousands of sites may be listed, they are often arranged alphabetically 10 - 15 per page, and so it is easy to reach the appropriate listings.

1 Enter the URL

4 Search for a keyword?

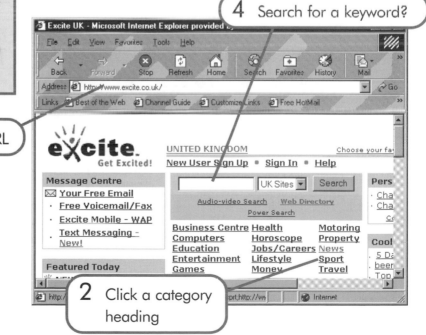

2 Click a category heading

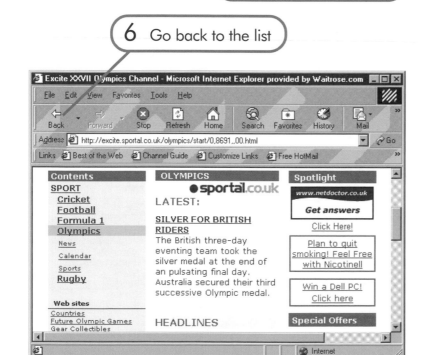

4 At any stage, enter key words if a box is provided to make a search of this sub-category.

5 When you reach the list of Web sites, page through.

6 Click any of interest, and use the Back button to return to the results list.

5 Scroll through the list

6 Go back to the list

Take note

Related Web pages transferred together onto the Internet form a *Web site*. The main address followed by / and then more information shows the exact page you are visiting on site.

Basic steps

1 Connect to the URL.

2 Click in the search box and enter your key words and symbols carefully.

3 Click the Search button (this may be labelled Go, Seek or Search), or press [Enter].

4 Work down through the list of Web sites pro- vided and, after visiting any, return to the list using the Back button.

Tip

Read the Help screens at the sites for advice about using key words with any particular search engine.

Search engines

Search engines build up huge databases of Web pages and you instruct them to carry out searches by matching *key words* you type into a special box – the query box.

The result is often vast lists of pages, but these start with the most relevant and each 'hit' will show the first line of contents and when the page was last updated, to help you decide whether to download and examine it in more detail.

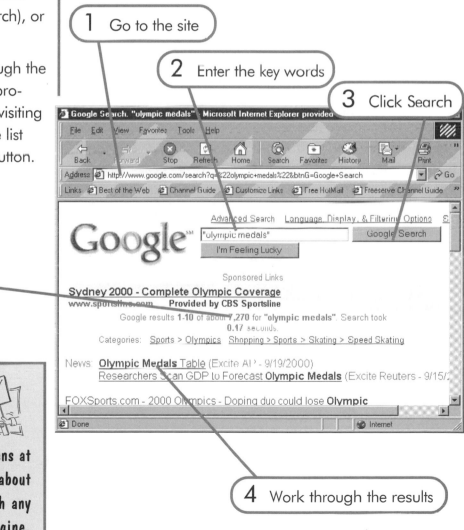

1 Go to the site

2 Enter the key words

3 Click Search

Number of pages found

4 Work through the results

Rules when entering key words:

- Type a phrase between quotation marks so that words are not searched independently, e.g. "Christmas Island" to avoid Christmas-based sites.

- Use logical operators or + or - signs so that a search will find sites that:

  Must contain all words joined by AND e.g. gardens AND Hampshire

  Can contain either word linked by OR

  Will be excluded if any words follow AND NOT

  Must contain words prefixed by +

  Must not contain words prefixed by -

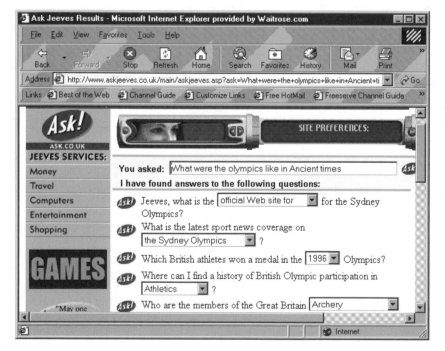

At some sites you can type in naturally worded questions – these are not generally the best way to get an exact match!

Favourite pages

❑ Adding Favorites

1 When you want to bookmark the current Web page, click Favorites.

2 Click Add… to open the Add Favorite dialog box.

3 Accept or amend the name so that you will recognise it when searching for it in future. (Automatic entries are often much too long or meaning-less).

4 Click on a folder for your page in the Create In window, or first create and name a new folder.

5 Click OK.

❑ To go to a favourite page, open the Favorites menu, open the folder and click on the page name.

After some time online, you may come across a web page that you know you will want to revisit. Rather than write down the exact URL on a piece of paper, you can save it into the browser's special filing system. This is known as *Favorites* in Internet Explorer and *Bookmarks* in Netscape.

Next time you want to access the page, open the Favorites menu, click the name and you will be taken directly to the page you 'bookmarked'.

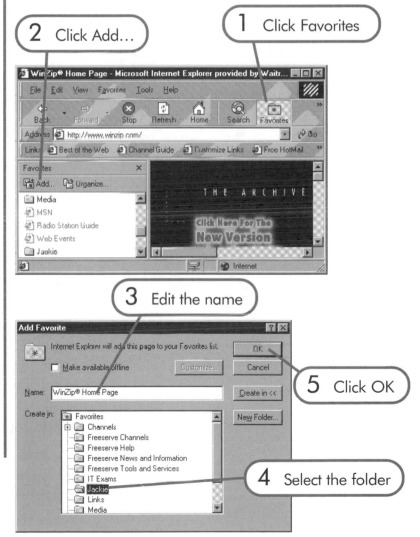

Organizing Favorites

To organize favourite pages, if they have been stored haphazardly, you can either use the folders provided (which may already contain numerous links included by your ISP), or create your own.

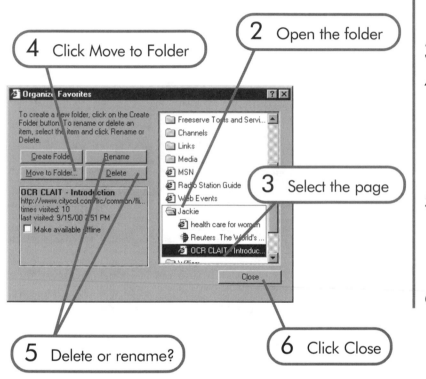

4 Click Move to Folder

2 Open the folder

3 Select the page

5 Delete or rename?

6 Click Close

- ❑ Organizing Favorites

1 Select Favorites – Organize

2 Scroll down to find the folder in which one was stored.

3 Select the named page.

4 To move it to a different folder, click Move to Folder and select the new destination folder in the window.

5 Choose other options if you want to delete or rename the page or create a new folder.

6 Click Close.

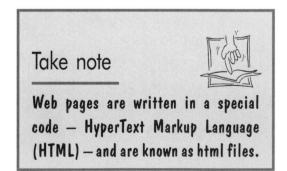

Take note

Web pages are written in a special code – HyperText Markup Language (HTML) – and are known as html files.

Going shopping

What do you want to buy today? A book, theatre tickets, holidays or a house? You can buy almost anything on the Internet nowadays, and it can be safe and much less tiring than walking round a real shopping centre.

As with any purchase, you must take certain precautions:

- Check the company exists – look for an address and phone number so there is someone to contact if you have a problem;

- Find out what they charge for delivery;

- Phone up the company when paying, if you don't trust the security system for taking credit card details on-line; and

- Make sure goods bought from overseas will work in the UK, e.g. are the videos the right type for your machine?

Research shows that people are often happiest dealing with companies with a high street presence or experience in the distribution of goods, but if you want to take the risk you could get a real bargain with a small, unknown organisation.

Tesco (www.tesco.co.uk) Having heavy shopping delivered can be a luxury worth far more than the current £5 delivery charge. Obtain the CD-ROM disk to load the 'virtual shop' and register your details, then browse the aisles, adding items to your trolley. When ready, place your order, select the delivery slot and wait for the doorbell.

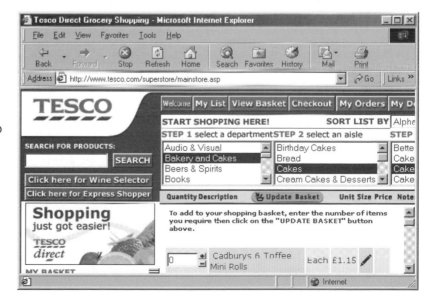

Printing Web pages

If you find a Web page you want to print, you can treat it in a similar fashion to a Word document. However, the length of a Web 'page' does not correspond to that of a word processed document, and may extend over several printed pages.

Many Web pages are divided into sections – *frames* – that comprise separate pages displayed in a special way. You need to take care when printing these to make sure you end up with the information you want.

Basic steps

1 To print one copy of the complete Web page, click the Print toolbar button.

2 To print a frame, click it first.

3 To change settings, go to File – Print.

4 For one frame, choose to print *Only the selected frame*.

5 To print only the first section of a long Web page, set the print range to Pages from 1–1.

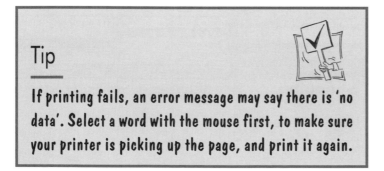

5 Set the print range

4 Only print the frame?

Tip

If printing fails, an error message may say there is 'no data'. Select a word with the mouse first, to make sure your printer is picking up the page, and print it again.

Basic steps

Saving

❏ Saving images

1 Right-click the image and select the Save Picture As... option.

2 Either leave the default file type, usually *jpg or gif*, or save it as a bitmap *(bmp)*.

3 Give it a name you will remember and click Save.

❏ Wallpapering

4 To have some fun, select Set As Wallpaper and have versions of Ihe picture as your Desktop background.

5 Return to normal via the Start – Settings – Control Panel – Display – Background – Wall-paper menu.

You save a Web page just like other documents. It will be saved as an html file and will open in the browser window. Images on Web pages may need to be saved separately as they are files in their own right.

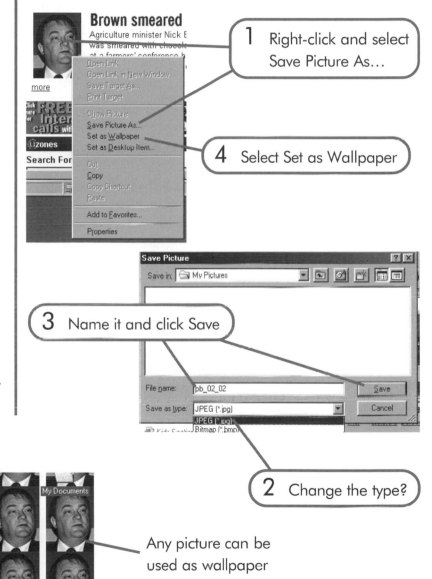

1 Right-click and select Save Picture As...

4 Select Set as Wallpaper

3 Name it and click Save

2 Change the type?

Any picture can be used as wallpaper

Downloading files

New versions of software, games or special Internet tools found on the Web can all be transferred and saved onto your computer by a process known as *downloading*. It can take a long time to complete the transfer, so you are best downloading at cheap rate times. Programs are often free, or trial versions which you pay for if you keep them permanently.

Follow downloading guidelines and stay connected to the Internet during transfer. At the end, you may need to restart your computer before you can use the new programs. You can usually choose a particular folder into which the files will be downloaded, and whether to place an icon on your desktop offering a shortcut to the program.

1 Go to the site where the file is located, e.g. www.winzip.com

2 Click the hyperlink to start the downloading process – it often just says <u>Click here</u>.

3 Accept the suggested location, or choose a folder in which to store your program.

4 A dialog box may be displayed showing the status of the transfer.

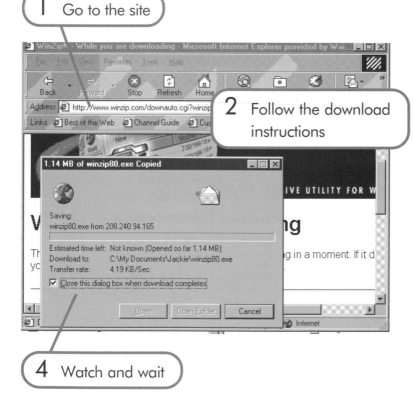

1 Go to the site

2 Follow the download instructions

4 Watch and wait

Take note

Commonly downloaded programs include document readers e.g. *Acrobat Adobe*, image editors e.g. *Paintshop Pro*, space savers that will compress your files e.g. *WinZip*, Web page authoring software e.g. *FrontPage Express* and software that allows you to transfer your own pages onto the Web e.g. CuteFTP.

What is e-mail?

E-mail is short for electronic mail and is a cheap and quick method for sending messages to other computer users via the Internet. Large documents or pictures can be sent in the form of attachments to your messages, and all you pay is a local phone charge.

Advantages over the post ('snail mail') or telephone:

- Messages sent to other countries arrive within minutes

- No need to be at home – messages wait in a distant mailbox until you download them onto your computer

- You'll never need to buy stamps or go to the postbox

E-mail addresses

You will need an e-mail address of your own, assigned when you register with an e-mail service, and the address of the person receiving your message. An e-mail address is made up of the following parts:

User name – this is chosen by you and is usually a nickname or combination of initials and surname, e.g. *z.nobody*

Mail server – the computer where your messages are held, *e.g. virgin.net*

These two parts are separated by @ so that the full address looks like this: *z.nobody@virgin.net*

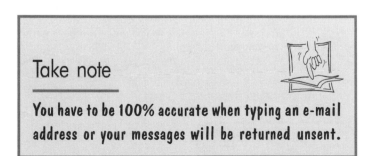

Outlook Express

The examples in this book relate to Microsoft Outlook Express version 5, but most e-mail systems work in a similar way. When you open the software (or register with a Web mail service, such as Microsoft's Hotmail) the main choices are:

- Opening an **Inbox** and viewing new messages;
- **Replying** to someone, or **forwarding** incoming messages to someone else;
- **Composing** new messages to send;
- Maintaining lists of addresses in your **Address Book**;
- Creating **folders** in which to store messages;
- Creating a special ending that you can add to messages automatically and which is known as a **signature**;
- **Attaching** a file to a message;
- **Deleting** unwanted messages.

Basic steps

1 Double-click your e-mail application icon to open the main window. This has toolbar options, tips and short cuts.

2 Click the Inbox folder to view your messages. (New users normally find a welcome message from their access provider.)

3 Select a message to see its contents in the lower preview pane.

4 To alter the size of any pane, click and drag its border when the mouse pointer shows a two-way arrow.

(1) Open the e-mail application

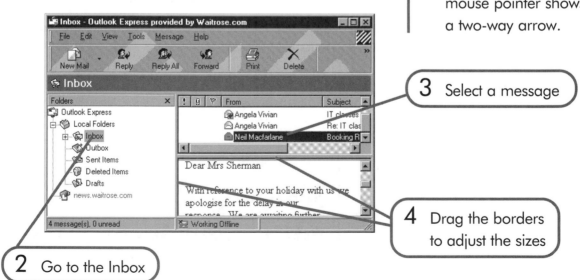

(3) Select a message

(2) Go to the Inbox

(4) Drag the borders to adjust the sizes

Basic steps

1 Click the New Mail button or select File – New – Mail Message.

2 Insert the relevant information.

3 Write your message.

4 Apply formatting and spell check it by clicking the Spelling button.

5 For an urgent message, select Priority – High. This will attach an exclamation mark to it.

6 Click Send to send it straight away, or select File – Send Later to retain it in the Outbox.

Tip

Take care when entering the Subject. Well-worded, it can ensure that your message stands out from many others that may be received and will be read rather than ignored.

Sending messages

To send a message, open a composing window and enter:

● The e-mail address of the recipient in the *To* box;

● The addresses of anyone receiving a copy in the *Cc.* box;

● The address of anyone who will receive a copy of the message unknown to other recipients – a blind copy – in the *Bcc.* box. (To use this box in Outlook Express version 5 you need to open it by selecting **View** – **All Headers**.)

● The subject of the message in the *Subject* box;

● The message itself, in the lower message box.

Either send your message straight away or keep it to send later when you go online.

In Outlook Express, messages are stored in the Outbox and, after sending, are listed in the Sent box.

> 6 Click Send

> 2 Insert the relevant information

> 5 Assign priority?

End of Term Party

File Edit View Insert Format Tools Message Help

Send Cut Copy Paste Undo Check Spelling Attach Priority

To: jane_mark@brookes.ac.uk

Cc:

Bcc:

Subject: End of Term Party

Arial 10 B U

Hi Jane

Thanks for the invitation. I'd love to come along.

> 4 Format and spell check

> 3 Write the message

Receiving messages

When you open Outlook Express, download new messages into your Inbox by clicking the Send/Receive and then the Connect buttons. Once messages appear, go offline to read and reply to them at your leisure.

For each message, you see exactly who sent it and when, and can print a hard copy if you want one. Each selected message opens in the preview pane, but double-click to open it fully.

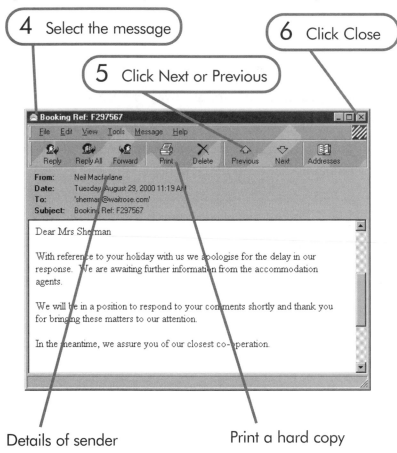

4 Select the message

5 Click Next or Previous

6 Click Close

Details of sender

Print a hard copy

Basic steps

1 Click the Send/Receive button to connect to your mail server and download any new messages waiting for you.

2 The number of messages will be displayed in brackets next to the Inbox.

3 If the Inbox is not your default opening screen, click this choice in the Folders pane to open it and view the messages.

4 Select a message to read in preview or open fully.

5 After reading the message, use Next or Previous buttons to read other messages.

6 Close its window with the Close button.

Basic steps

1 Select the incoming
message and click the
Reply button ![Reply]. A
composing window will
open showing the To:
box completed and the
Subject: box starting
Re: followed by the
original subject.

2 Partially or fully delete
the original message,
or leave as a reminder.

3 Click in the space at the
top of the message box
and type in your reply.

4 Complete and send
exactly as you would
any original message.

2 Edit the original
message

Replying

To reply to the author of a message, using the **Reply** function
will automatically enter their address and give you the chance
to retain some or all the original message in your own reply.

Forward a message to a third person by clicking the **Forward**
button ![Forward] and completing the message box as normal. The
Subject box will include the original subject prefixed by *Fw:*
but you will need to enter the new e-mail address yourself.

4 Complete and send

To: and Subject
completed for you

Re: Booking Ref: F297567

File Edit View Insert Format Tools Message Help

Send   Cut   Copy   Paste   Undo   Check   Spelling   Attach   Priority   Sign

To: Neil Macfarlane
Cc:
Subject: Re: Booking Ref: F297567

Dear Neil

Thanks for your message, I am delighted that
----- Original Message -----
From: Neil Macfarlane
To: <sherman@waitrose.com>
Sent: Tuesday, August 29, 2000 11:19 AM
Subject: Booking Ref: F297567

>
> Our Ref: CS4446\NSM

3 Type your reply

Tip

**If you are one of a number of people sent a message and want
everyone on the mailing list to receive a copy of your reply, click
the *Reply All* button rather than the *Reply* button. The e-mail
addresses of the whole group will be included in the *To:* box.**

Attaching files

Although you can use basic formatting tools, you can't send beautifully word-processed e-mail messages, or insert pictures. Instead, you should attach these as files created and saved elsewhere. They will remain in their original state and will be opened by your message recipient into an application.

Basic steps

❑ Attaching a file

1 Click the Attach toolbar button [Attach] or select Insert – File Attachment.

2 In the Insert Attachment dialog box, browse through your folders and select the file you want to send.

3 Click the Attach button. The filename will be shown in a new Attach box.

4 Repeat the process to attach several files to a single message.

5 To delete an attachment, select it and press [Delete].

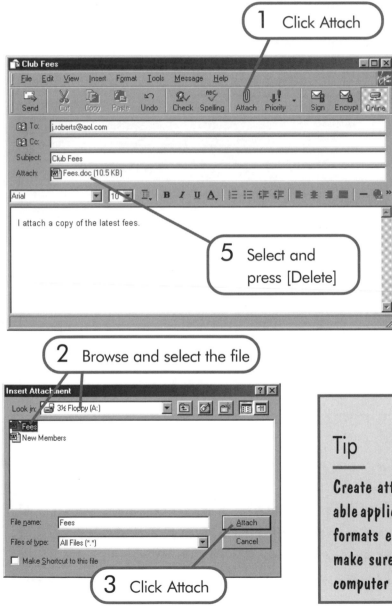

1 Click Attach

5 Select and press [Delete]

2 Browse and select the file

3 Click Attach

Tip

Create attachments using commonly available applications, or save them in simplified formats e.g. file type .rtf (rich text), to make sure people using different types of computer can open and view them.

Basic steps

1 A paperclip icon next to a new message shows there is an attachment.

2 Select the message.

Either

3 Click the paperclip in the top right-hand corner of the preview pane, then click on the filename.

Or

4 Double-click the filename showing in the Attach box after opening the message fully.

5 Click Save Attachments to save it elsewhere.

Opening attachments

Messages with attachments display a paperclip icon. Open the attached file to view it, or save it if you want to transfer it to a different machine or keep it with related files.

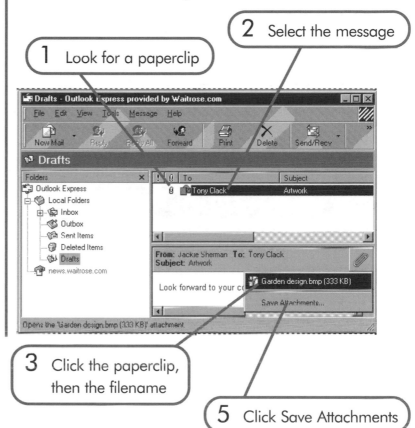

2 Select the message

1 Look for a paperclip

3 Click the paperclip, then the filename

5 Click Save Attachments

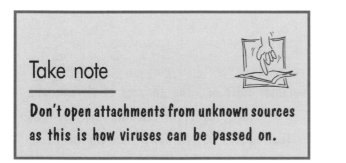

Take note

Don't open attachments from unknown sources as this is how viruses can be passed on.

137

The Address Book

It would be quite annoying if you had to enter the same details every time you sent a message, and so you are saved the trouble by being able to build up an address book of e-mail addresses. You can also organize group mailing lists so that entering the group name inserts all the separate addresses at once.

1 Open the Address Book

2 Select New – New Contact

5 Store other details?

Address Book - Jacqueline Sher...

File Edit View Tools Help

New   Properties Delete   Find People Print
New Contact...   h list:
New Group...
New Folder...   E-Mail Address   Business Phone   Home Phone

Creates a new cor

Daisy Green Properties   ? X

Name | Home | Business | Personal | Other | NetMeeting | Digital IDs

Enter name and e-mail information about this contact here.

First: Daisy   Middle: Last: Green

Title: Display: Daisy Green   Nickname:

E-Mail Addresses: d.green@compuserve.com   Add

d.green@compuserve.com (Default E-Mail)   Edit

                                                 Remove

                                                 Set as Default

3 Give the name and e-mail address

4 Edit the display name

                        OK   Cancel

6 Click OK

Basic steps

1 In the Outlook Express window, click the Addresses button or select Tools – Address Book.

2 Click New and select New Contact.

3 Complete the name and e-mail details and click Add. The address will appear in the main window.

4 Accept or amend the name to be displayed.

5 Click other tabs to store more information.

6 Click OK.

❑ To group several addresses under a single heading, select New – New Group.

Tip

You can automatically add the address of anyone who sends you a message, by right-clicking the sender's name and selecting **Add To Address Book** from the menu.

1 Click the book symbol next to To: or Cc: to open the Address Book list.

2 Select a person or group name in the left pane.

3 Click the To:, Cc: or Bcc: buttons to enter the address into the appropriate message box.

4 Click OK and you will return to your message.

5 To delete an address, open the Address Book, select the name and click Delete.

Once you have built up a list of e-mail addresses in your Address Book, you can enter these automatically into your new messages.

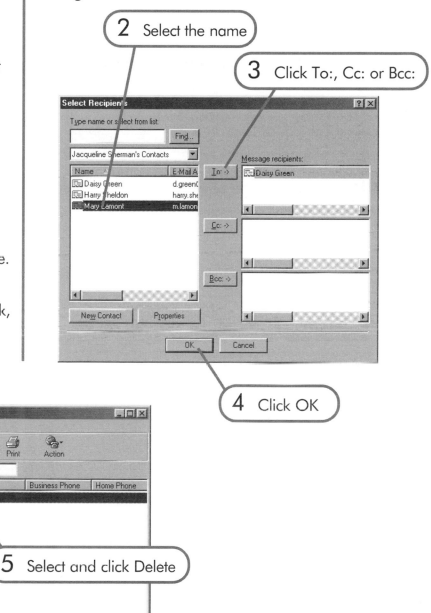

Organizing messages

All new messages appear in your Inbox, but you should use existing folders or create new ones to store your messages systematically. Just as with file management, referring to a particular message is then much easier as you only need to look in a suitably named folder.

Basic steps

1 Click the folder in which you want your new one to be created

2 Select File – Folder – New.

3 Enter the name for your new folder in the box.

4 The 'parent' folder will be selected in the list. Leave or amend this choice and click OK.

5 Click the + next to a folder name to see its new subfolder.

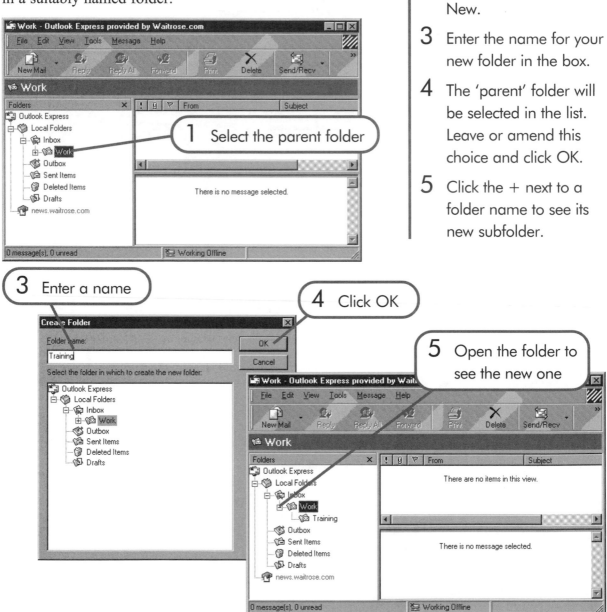

1 Select the parent folder

3 Enter a name

4 Click OK

5 Open the folder to see the new one

Moving messages

1 Select the message.

2 Open the Edit menu and select Move to or Copy to Folder.

3 Select the destination folder, or create a new one first, and click OK.

Or

4 Display both the message and destination folder on the screen.

5 Drag the message across to the destination folder. (Hold down [Control] to copy but not move the original.)

6 When the folder becomes highlighted, let go the mouse.

Once you have created folders in which to store your messages, you can file the messages you want to keep. You can also delete any you know you won't need by selecting them and clicking the Delete button.

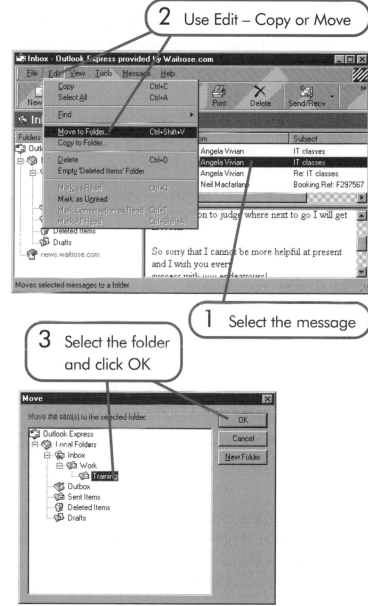

2 Use Edit – Copy or Move

1 Select the message

3 Select the folder and click OK

Tip

If you delete a message by mistake, open the *Deleted items* folder and drag the message out into another folder.

Summary

❑ The Internet links computers around the world. Register with an ISP to access it via a modem and the telephone system, and view it through a browser.

❑ Web pages are written in a special code that allows you to click on text or images – a hyperlink – and link up with other pages. The address of any page is known as its URL.

❑ Searching the Web is aided by using directories or search engines. These allow you to search for key words or to work through sites that have been grouped together under common headings.

❑ Whenever you find a page you will want to revisit, you can bookmark it by adding its URL to a list of links to favourite Web addresses.

❑ Shopping on the Internet is becoming as normal as mail order, and as long as you take sensible precautions, should be simple, safe and may save money.

❑ You can print and save pages and images from the Web, and you download programs onto your PC.

❑ Once you have registered with an ISP, you can send e-mails around the world for the cost of a local phone call.

❑ Documents and images can be sent by e-mail as attached files.

❑ People's e-mail addresses can be saved into an Address Book and added to your messages automatically, and you can organize messages in folders just as you organize your own files.

Index